Mary Taylor Simeti is a native New York who [illegible] forty years. She and her husband run his family's farm, where they produce wine and olive oil. A regular contributor to the travel section of the *New York Times*, her other books are the acclaimed *On Persephone's Island, Sicilian Food* and *Travels with a Medieval Queen*.

Maria Grammatico's pastry shop, the Pasticceria Maria Grammatico, can be found on via Vittorio Emanuele in Erice, Sicily. *Bitter Almonds* is an invitation to experience its delicacies.

BITTER ALMONDS

'Spirited and often moving . . . A unique and special book'
Library Journal

'Very little can measure up to an intense, well-written meditation on one human being's past . . . A window on a way of life that has vanished'
Journal of Italian Food & Wine

'Nothing less than remarkable'
Washington Post

'Mary Taylor Simeti is a gifted cook, a gifted oral historian, and most importantly, a gifted writer with great respect for her subject . . . Whether for cultural insight, for recipes that will turn your kitchen into a traditional Sicilian bakery, or simply for a good read, *Bitter Almonds* is a book that should not be missed'
Cook's Illustrated

'No-one brings Sicily to life for us quite like Maria Taylor Simeti. *Bitter Almonds* introduces Sicilian baker Maria Grammatico, a woman of such engaging warmth, wisdom and grit that even if you don't cook (and her food is superb), you will find her and the book irresistible'
Lynne Rossetto Kasper, author of *The Italian Country Table*

Maria at the Istituto San Carlo, circa 1959

BITTER ALMONDS

RECOLLECTIONS AND RECIPES FROM
A SICILIAN GIRLHOOD

MARY TAYLOR SIMETI
& MARIA GRAMMATICO

BANTAM BOOKS

LONDON · NEW YORK · TORONTO · SYDNEY · AUCKLAND

BITTER ALMONDS: RECOLLECTIONS AND RECIPES FROM A SICILIAN
GIRLHOOD
A BANTAM BOOK : 0 553 81465 6

First published in New York by William Morrow and Company Inc.

PRINTING HISTORY
Bantam Books edition published 2002

1 3 5 7 9 10 8 6 4 2

Set in 10/14.5pt Sabon by
Phoenix Typesetting, Burley-in-Wharfedale, West Yorkshire.

Bantam Books are published by Transworld Publishers,
61–63 Uxbridge Road, London W5 5SA,
a division of The Random House Group Ltd,
in Australia by Random House Australia (Pty) Ltd,
20 Alfred Street, Milsons Point, Sydney, NSW 2061, Australia,
in New Zealand by Random House New Zealand Ltd,
18 Poland Road, Glenfield, Auckland 10, New Zealand
and in South Africa by Random House (Pty) Ltd,
Endulini, 5a Jubilee Road, Parktown 2193, South Africa.

Printed and bound in Great Britain by
Clays Ltd, St Ives plc.

'Facciamo tutto a mano, partendo dalle sostanze naturali, dal latte, dalle zucche, dalle mandorle, ai pistacchi. I costi delle materie prime oggi sono proibitivi ed esigui sono i margini di guadagno. Svolgiamo questa attività per tenere aperta una finestra, sia pure protetta da grate, sul mondo che non ci è ostile e che dobbiamo pur amare.'

'We do everything by hand, starting with natural ingredients, from the milk and the squashes to the almonds and pistachios. The cost of the raw materials today is prohibitive, and the margins of profit are very narrow. We continue this activity so that we may maintain a window open – albeit protected by an iron grate – on the world, which is not hostile to us and which we have, after all, to love.'

From an interview with a Benedictine nun, Palermo, *Il Giornale di Sicilia*, 5 October 1981

Contents

Preface

I consider it an honour to have been the recipient of Maria Grammatico's friendship and of her reminiscences, and I hope that in putting her story and her recipes on paper I have done them justice. For purposes of narration I cut and rearranged the transcriptions of my interviews with Maria before translating them, but I have added nothing that Maria herself has not said to me on one occasion or another.

I would like to emphasize that this is *her* story, and it tells of life in the Istituto San Carlo as *she* remembers it, her memories coloured by the circumstances of her entrance into the institute and by the way in which her personality reacted to its strictures. Had I listened to Ninetta or to Titì, I would probably have been given a somewhat different picture. The isolated and repetitive quality of life at the San Carlo has also blurred Maria's sense of the passage of time; she has a poor memory for dates and the chronology of her story is occasionally shaky. I have been as exact as possible within the limits of the material at hand, but have always felt that it would be neither correct nor necessary for me to run outside checks on what Maria has told me.

Maria and I are extremely grateful to Susan Derecskey, unsung power behind many cookbooks and official recipe tester in the United States for this endeavour. Her enthusiasm and encouragement for our project and her professional skill and scrupulousness, both in testing and in writing the recipes, have made an enormous contribution.

We would also like to thank Professor Vincenzo Adragna of the Biblioteca Comunale of Erice, who has been very generous with his time and with his extensive knowledge of Erice's history, and Nino Privitera, for allowing us to reproduce the mono photographs he took inside the Istituto San Carlo in the early 1970s.

Finally, we would like to thank Maria's brother, Leonardo Grammatico, whose contribution goes well beyond the interview recorded here; he has been as supportive of this book as he has been of all of Maria's undertakings.

MARY TAYLOR SIMETI

Bitter Almonds

I

A fresh almond pastry, dusted with powdered sugar or coated with chocolate, has been a part of every trip to Erice for almost as far back as I can remember. I couldn't have eaten one on my first visit, of course: when I came to Sicily in 1962, just out of college and ready for a year of volunteer development work, Maria Grammatico was still closed up in the Istituto San Carlo, the convent-like orphanage where she spent all of her adolescence. Her pastry shop didn't exist, and I didn't know enough then about Sicily to realize that there were convents where you could give your order to a dim figure behind an iron grate and place your money upon a 'wheel', a revolving hatch that slid the coins through the wall and brought out pastries in their stead.

It was an austere world that I encountered upon my arrival in Sicily. The first half of the twentieth century had done little to leaven the extreme poverty bequeathed by centuries of foreign conquest and domination, a poverty that, if anything, had been exacerbated by the economic policies of the Fascist regime and by the Second World War. If the city of Trapani, the major seaport on the west coast of the island, had undergone a degree of modernization in the preceding decades, followed by a degree of bomb damage during the Allied invasion in 1943, in the lonely farms of Trapani's hinterland and in the little town of Erice, hovering on a mountaintop above the city, little had changed. Daily life continued much as it had in the nineteenth century.

In the early 1960s the effects of the economic boom that was transforming Northern Italy were just beginning to trickle down to Sicily. In subsequent years, a wave of prosperity and modern technology descended, altering the face of the countryside and rendering the inhabitants of Sicily's towns and cities more or less indistinguishable from anyone else in Southern Europe. The world in which Maria Grammatico had grown up all but disappeared.

The story behind the almond pastries was slow to reveal itself. In an account of a trip to Erice in the early 1980s, I wrote in passing of purchasing 'Erice's special almond cakes in a pastry shop just off the main square' but devoted much more space to describing the classical origins and the abundant flora of this medieval village, whose spectacular location, on the top of a solitary mountain that rises 2,400 feet above the coastal plain, has inevitably attracted myth and speculation. Thucydides claimed that Erice and her sister city, Segesta, were founded in the twelfth century BC by Trojans escaping from the fall. These descendants of Æneas became known as the Elymians, and they were one of the three peoples that inhabited Sicily when the Greeks began to colonize the island in the eighth century BC.

Archaeological data confirm the Eastern Mediterranean, most probably Anatolian origin of the Elymians, but as of yet, nothing has been found that establishes the date of their arrival in western Sicily. It is probable, however, that they found a goddess already installed. The Great Mother of the Mediterranean Basin has been worshipped at Erice since time immemorial. The Carthaginians called her Astarte; the Greeks knew her as Aphrodite, and claimed that the lady had risen from the waves just below the sacred mountain, had lain on its slopes with an Argonaut, Butes 'the Beekeeper', and had given birth there to the king of the Elymians, Eryx, whose name means heather. Daedalus dedicated a honeycomb wrought of gold to Aphrodite's altar at Erice, and the Romans lay with sacred prostitutes at the shrine of Venus Ericina.

It is to be expected that so ancient a tradition would be slow to die, yet it is nonetheless astonishing to read that vestiges of the pagan cult were still to be found in the sixteenth century. A document dated 1554 states that the mid-August festivities in honour of the Assumption of the Virgin Mary were established by papal order 'to distract the large flow of people coming to the temple of Venus'. In the second half of that century, a portrait of the Virgin was miraculously saved from a shipwreck and placed in the nearby town of Custonaci, and in the following years the Madonna of Custonaci gradually displaced Aphrodite as the patron saint of Erice. There are those who claim that something still persists: Erice's traditional wedding biscuits, known as *miliddi*, are said to descend from *mylloi*, the ritual cakes sweetened with honey and sacred to the goddess that are described in the poetry of Theocritus.

My curiosity about the later periods of Erice's history was whetted by a 1985 trip to see *I Misteri*, the Good Friday processions that take place on a grandiose scale in Trapani, and on a much smaller, more intimate scale in Erice itself.

Here my sister and I followed the almost life-sized statues representing the Passion of Christ and the Sorrows of the Madonna, a Renaissance reworking of the mystery plays of the Middle Ages, through narrow cobbled streets, past abandoned churches, medieval houses, and baroque mansions. The mist that floated in from the Mediterranean, curling under the arches and around the bell towers, seemed to cut us off from the modern world below and project us backwards in time to the period of Erice's second flowering, when the town became known as Monte San Giuliano. (The classical name was restored by Mussolini.) Almost completely deserted in the Byzantine and Arab eras, Erice owed its rebirth and subsequent wealth to the lands assigned to it by the Norman King William II in the twelfth century, a grant reconfirmed in the following century by the Holy Roman Emperor Frederick II. These vast communal territories, which were not carved up definitively until the middle of the nineteenth century, nurtured a flourishing middle class, which built itself miniature mountaintop palaces in which to escape the heat of the Sicilian summer. Hoping perhaps to escape the heat of eternal perdition as well, it also endowed some forty-two churches and a number of convents and orphanages. Yet the prosperity of Monte San Giuliano did not survive the dismembering of its territory. The buildings still stand, but the doors of many are boarded up and their roofs are falling; only a handful of resident faithful remain to follow Erice's processions.

The Good Friday procession disbanded just a few steps from Maria's pastry shop. We entered in search of something to warm us up and were greeted by a counter full of marzipan lambs. Unlike most of the paschal lambs on sale throughout

Sicily at Eastertime, which are made in standard moulds that vary only in size and portray the lamb sitting in a grassy pasture, Maria's lambs were lying down. Eyes open, tongues hanging out a bit, fleece beautifully executed curl by curl, they gave little clue to the fact that they represented the sacrificial, slaughtered lamb.

By that time I was doing the research for a second book, a history of Sicilian food, in which a chapter was to be dedicated to the pastries traditionally made in convents throughout the island. To my knowledge, no thorough study of this tradition has been made: cultural anthropology in Sicily, perhaps because of its ideological matrix, appears to concentrate on the peasantry and to take less interest in institutions, especially those, such as convents, that were religious in nature and often aristocratic in origin. And historians of the church are perhaps uncomfortable with – or at least uninterested in – an aspect of convent life that is almost totally devoid of religious content. Even before making pastries to sell became a source of income for the convents, pastries as gifts were an acceptable currency by which the cloister could purchase the attention of the outside world, a tray of marzipan or almond cakes in exchange for a visit and a bit of gossip.

Early reference to convent pastries in Sicily reflect the ambivalence of the Church towards this activity. At the end of the sixteenth century, the nuns of the Diocese of Mazara del Vallo were forbidden to make *cassata* during Holy Week, that they might not be distracted from their prayers. Yet some fifty years later the manufacture of marzipan and other sweets was a monopoly awarded to the *monache di casa*, self-appointed celibates living at home, so as to ensure them '*lo honesto vivere*' – an honest income.

However much earlier the tradition may have begun, by the end of the eighteenth century the manufacture of pastries in the convents was extremely widespread, flourishing in some cases beyond the limits of propriety. After the unification of Italy in 1860 and the confiscation of the Church's properties, many convents closed, and others were forced to make the pastry trade one of their principal sources of income. In the years since the Second World War, the number of convents that produce pastries has dropped abruptly: the elderly nuns are dying and the new recruits, when they can be found, are no longer attracted to this sort of activity. The one nun capable of making the exquisite marzipan grapes I described in my first book, *On Persephone's Island*, had taken her secrets with her to the grave before I completed the second book, and other such recipes are disappearing unrecorded across the island.

I did not immediately connect Maria's lamb, lying on a tray surrounded by flower-topped cakes known as *pasta di conserva*, with Carlo Levi's description of buying pastries at a convent in Erice in 1951: 'The pastries appeared on the wheel, tender flowers of green and pink and violet and azure.' But from a purely visual standpoint, the lamb was memorable, and when in 1988 the American Craft Museum asked me to procure them examples of Sicilian sugar work for a show to be dedicated to 'The Confectioner's Art', I immediately returned to Erice.

It was in the course of negotiating for a first lamb, which eventually began to ooze its citron preserves, and later for a second, jam-free, lamb to go on tour, that I became friendly with Maria and began to hear about how she had learned to make pastries as an orphan in the Istituto San Carlo. Maria loves to tell stories, and she is worldly enough to know which details of her early life seem the most exotic to a contemporary American. I was rapidly hooked: each return to Erice revealed another anecdote, some new Dickensian detail of life in the orphanage, or some long-forgotten recipe. The following winter I persuaded *Gourmet* magazine to commission an article about Maria's almond pastries, and I began to visit her in earnest, armed with notebook and tape recorder.

The article was published in 1991, but the visits have continued. Now that this book is finished, I no longer have an excuse to tape our meetings, yet I can hardly bear for Maria to open her mouth when the tape recorder isn't running. She speaks when reminiscing in the strong and musical dialect of her youth, with the lilt, the epithet, and the recurring refrain of the oral storytelling tradition. Her language is slightly old-fashioned, uncontaminated by the mass media, but every so often she injects a very contemporary concept, a reminder that this is not some relic of the past who is speaking, but an artist who is also a sharp businesswoman and a successful entrepreneur. Much of the beauty of her speech is lost in my translation, but the world she describes would, I believe, be fascinating in any language.

After the war we went hungry, we truly went hungry. In Sicily it was like some primitive time. I can remember, as a child, where I lived someone died almost every day, every single day, and if anyone passed by they walked right over him. A lot has changed in Sicily, you see, and I have worked very,

very hard, I've made it all on my own. I was eleven when I entered the institute. I had no choice but to work.

I started in right away. I'd already had a little schooling, through fourth grade. So I was put to work. My little sister Angela, who was only six when we entered the San Carlo, was sent to school through fifth grade, that's all. Nothing more; women didn't go to school.

The San Carlo was over there where the Salerniana is, where they have the exhibitions. But it was much bigger then, it went all along the Via San Carlo, as far as the Porta Ercole gate.

Do you know where La Pentolaccia restaurant is? That was part of the San Carlo, too. That's where the machines were. During the war they couldn't make any more pastries, there wasn't any flour, there wasn't any sugar, and the nuns began to spin wool to make sweaters with, to make socks, and they sold them to earn their living. So they spun wool. There were all these spinning machines, hand ones though, made of wood, with a pedal. You pedalled with your foot and that turned a crank, and the yarn came out.

Above the restaurant were the dormitories, where we slept. The nuns too: they had their beds behind a screen. In my room there were me and my sister and two nuns. Then in the next room there were eight beds plus two for the nuns, you see. In another there were three or four. That's how it was.

When I entered the San Carlo there were about fifteen nuns, and then about sixteen or seventeen orphans. We were the littlest. My sister and I, then Nuccia, and Maria Franchini – we were the youngest. Then there was Maria, there was Ninetta, there was the other one, Serenedda. There was Titì. But Titì was already older, she was four years older than me, and she didn't have a big girl in charge of her, because she'd already been there for four years. Anna was big when she came in, Anna was about nineteen, I think. They could leave when they wanted, but not before they were twenty-one – when they came of age. In fact, Maria left later on, she got married and left, Serenedda left too, Nuccia left, Anna left . . .

But the one I couldn't stand was one of the big girls. Titì. Titì and I were like cat and dog, because Titì was four years older, and she wanted me to call her ma'am, and even today, if we meet in the middle of the street, I still call her ma'am. She was older, she'd already been there four years, and that made her feel important. I was always quarrelling with her. Even with the others she was always bossy, even with Ninetta. How she and Ninetta fought! Because Titì was – perhaps Titì wasn't really mean, but she liked to think she was important.

So all in all, when I got there there were about thirty-three of us, plus the 'Auntie'. There was a lady, an Auntie, who did all the outside work. She came in the morning, she went to do the shopping, she accompanied my sister to school; if they needed a cauliflower she bought the cauliflower, if they needed greens she bought the greens, if they needed a packet of butter she bought the packet of butter, and then she'd sweep the courtyard. And the Auntie swept outside the parlatory, where the wheel for the pastries is – that the Auntie had to sweep: we couldn't go out there. Then we cooked lunch, the Auntie took her share and went home. She came back again about three o'clock, to see if they wanted anything, if there was anything else to buy, any other errand to do. And she was paid by the ECA, the Auntie was. The Auntie would go out to shop, but for Angela and me she never bought anything; because we didn't have any money, there was nothing we could buy.

The Auntie had to do all the outside work because the nuns didn't go out. Before, the San Carlo was a cloistered convent, and then, during the war, Mussolini took away all its property and left it as a lay institute. And it was administered by the ECA, the town welfare agency. After the war no more nuns entered, and the ones who were there remained there just as they were: there were nuns there who had entered when they were five or six years old and had never left that convent.

There was our Mother Superior, the Administrator, who was of a rare beauty. I knew her when she was an old woman, but when she was young she must have been very, very beautiful. '*Ministra*', we called her. She entered the institute because she was an only child, and her mother and father had died. She was of good position and had a guardian to administer all her property. The guardian had to decide where this young lady should go and stay, and he took her to the nuns. At eighteen, no, at twenty-one, because in those days it was twenty-one, she had to choose whether to leave the convent and start a family; but she didn't want to leave, she stayed there. And she didn't enter because she had a vocation, she entered just because they brought her there.

There were at least fifteen nuns: the two Fontana sisters, and that's two, and another two, Suor Agnese and Suor What's-her-name, and that's four, Ministra five, Suor Luigia six, Suor Serafina seven, Suor Maria Angela, Suor Stellina, then there was another, who died three months after we got there – and then who was there? In my room there was Suor

22

Stellina, and the Ministra, then Suor Serafina and Suor Agnese, and then on this side there were Suor Benedetta and Suor Ninuccia, in the first room, and then in the big room Suor Domitilla, Suor Concetta, Suor Teresa – did I count Suor Luisa? – and Suor Angelica, too.

There weren't any new nuns, ever. There was one who – wait a minute, she was the one who was bedridden for twelve years. Twelve years – Suor Benedetta! She was a nun from the Convent of Santa Teresa. When that convent closed, they brought her to the San Carlo. And then there was another one, I think it was Suor Angelica, who came from the Convent of San Salvatore. When they closed those convents and there wasn't anybody left, they brought them to the San Carlo, these two nuns. One from Santa Teresa and one from San Salvatore.

At Santa Teresa they made flowers, the ones they put around the wax Baby Jesuses, the ones in bell jars? Suor Benedetta used to make the flowers out of the resin from almond trees. She melted it and mixed it with wheat starch and colours. Instead, at San Salvatore the nuns did embroidery – what they call *filetto*, drawn thread embroidery – and then they also made pastries to sell. It was Suor Angelica, who came from San Salvatore, who knew how to make *genovesi* (16)* and taught us how. They were her speciality. But she made the *pasta frolla* (3) dough with lard, that's what they used in those days, the kind of lard the butcher made. It was pork fat that was rendered and filtered and put in a can. That's what they'd buy to make biscuits, to make pasta frolla; they used this because in those days it wasn't as if there

* Refers to recipe number. See table of contents for page numbers.

was margarine. But then it wasn't that they sold that many genovesi then either, it wasn't like today.

At the San Carlo, pastries were on sale every day – but not everything. We sold little cakes of marzipan called pasta di conserva, but all the other things that we made out of almond paste (*pasta di mandorla*, 1) were made on special order. Like, oh, I don't know, the paschal lambs were made on order, the marzipan fruit too, the *frutta di Martorana* (7), because otherwise we got left with all this Martorana. In those days people only bought it for All Souls' Day; nowadays we make it all year long, but then no, only at the beginning of November. The paschal lambs were for Easter, for Christmas the hearts, and the Baby Jesuses in their cradles.

You make almond paste with almonds that have been shelled and skinned. We used to grind them in a hand-cranked meat grinder, a big one. After the almonds were ground, we'd weigh out the sugar and the water and cook them together. When the sugar syrup makes a thick thread, you throw in the almonds, and you stir it all together well over the heat. When we took it off the stove, we'd pour it out onto the marble table. And while it was still warm, we began to knead it with heavy rolling pins: we'd work it and work it until we'd kneaded it into a smooth paste, because it wasn't as if there were machines to knead it then.

And so you had almond paste and you'd model it in plaster Martorana moulds, in the shape of whatever fruit you wanted – peach, pear, apple, apricot. Then you had to dry it: to dry it, you'd put it into big wooden chests, the kind of chests you used to use for linen? On the sides of these chests there were strips of wood that held up big net-bottomed trays, like sieves but specially made.

24

'We'd put all the Martorana fruit in these trays to dry . . .'

We'd put all the Martorana fruit in these trays to dry, and underneath, in the bottom of the chest, we'd put *cuffune*, earthenware braziers with just enough burning embers in them to dry out the fruit. For about two days, with a very, very slow fire.

And then we painted the fruit: we'd give them a first coat, a base coat of yellow, and put them to dry again – because in those days there was always mist here, months of mist, and nothing would ever dry properly. And it wasn't as if we had stoves or anything, no wood stoves, nothing like that. So cold you could die! To get warm at the San Carlo we used to put cuffune in our beds, cuffune with wicker domes over them, and that way we warmed our beds.

We used vegetable colourings to paint the marzipan, store-bought ones, and sometimes, if we ran out, we used terra rossa, the red pigment that housepainters use to colour stucco with, and Suor Stellina would mix a tiny bit of this with a little white lead and she'd paint the cheeks on the apricots, on the peaches.

The Christmas hearts were made of the same paste: you put *conserva di cedro* (30) – citron preserves – in the middle and cover it with another sheet of paste and then you decorate it with leaves and roses, and you can even put a Baby Jesus in the centre. We used to make the Baby Jesuses ourselves, there was a special mould. And to make the paste for the Baby Jesus come whiter, we'd add a little sugar – at the San Carlo we called it 'sugar on the slab'. It was like fondant sugar. You couldn't buy it ready-made in those days, so we'd make sugar-on-the-slab ourselves. You cook water and sugar and when it makes a thick thread, good and thick, you pour it onto a marble slab and then with a spatula you work it around and around and around, and it gets whiter and whiter – like an icing. And we'd put a little of this in the almond paste to make it whiter. And then a little bit of red colouring, just a tiny bit, to give it a flesh colour. And if there wasn't any colouring, then we'd put a little bit of terra rossa in the paste, but ever so little. And then you painted them; Suor Stellina, that is, she'd paint the diaper on the Baby Jesus, and give him eyes and pink cheeks. Suor Stellina had hands of gold for this work. Hands of gold she had; the rest of us are just poor imitations of her.

The lambs were all made by hand; there weren't any moulds for them then. I was the first one to make a mould. Suor Teresa made the body, and she filled it with conserva, and she made the legs, Suor Stellina painted the faces, and we girls put the wool on. But not like we do today, using a pastry bag. We used to make each curl with our fingers, one by one.

'The lambs were all made by hand; there weren't any moulds for them then.' Suor Maria Angela (*left*) and Suor Stellina at work.

'Suor Stellina painted the faces, and we girls put the wool on . . .'

Have you ever seen any of the old kind, the kind we used to make? Last year I didn't make any at all, but this year I'd like to make one, just one, just for the pleasure of it. It takes so much time! It's a dying tradition; the only ones who know how to do it are me, Ninetta, and Titì. Not even my sister Angela. Suor Stellina taught me, she'd make a mark with the knife where each curl was to go, and give me a lump of paste, and I'd kneel beside her and make the curls and put them on. But if it's something that you have within yourself, something that you love to do . . .

They made the moulds for the Martorana themselves, with plaster, but there weren't as many different kinds as there are today. They didn't have bananas: I'd never even seen one, to tell you the truth. I never saw a banana before I left the San Carlo. We made peaches, pears, apples, apricots, pomegranates – Suor Stellina made a beautiful pomegranate, split open with the seeds showing – and then mushrooms and chestnuts, peeled chestnuts and whole chestnuts. This was the Martorana fruit that people gave as presents for All Souls' Day, you give it to children as presents from the dead. Us? We'd each get one piece of fruit, and a couple of burnt cinnamon biscuits, if there were any. We girls used to burn some on purpose.

Mostly we sold cinnamon biscuits, the ones called *mostaccioli di Erice* (23). Then pasta di conserva, and *bocconcini* (12), almond bites, a few *amaretti* (28), and that's all. Pasta di conserva are little shells of almond paste that are filled with preserves and decorated with marzipan flowers. Then they get covered with a special icing that you use on almond paste and put in the oven, just enough to dry them, in a very, very low oven. That puts a shine on them.

In convent dialect we called this sugar icing *cilepro*. You take a kilo of sugar and cook it with half a litre of water until it reaches the thin thread stage, and then you take it off the fire. Then you beat it, either with a beater or by hand, with a stick of *ferla*, not wood, ferla. It's sort of like cork, but it's called ferla.* Because ferla won't absorb on you. Ferla doesn't absorb anything at all. And you keep beating it, around and around and around, until it turns white. At the San Carlo we'd cook twelve kilos of sugar at a time and we had to beat it for six or seven hours before it turned white.

And then for feast days we used to make – let's see, for All Souls' Day we made Martorana, for Christmas we made the Baby Jesuses, the hearts with the Baby Jesuses, for Easter paschal lambs and *cassate siciliane* (44) – it all depended on the feast day. For Christmas we used to make *biscotti al fico* (22) too, pastries with dried figs in them, and honey and almonds, and orange peel as well. And then there was something called *rametti di miele*, honey branches; you made a dough of semolina flour and honey. That's all there was in it. And then this dough got shaped like flowering branches, like the ones they make out of bread for St Joseph's Day? All flowery. And then I think we used to sprinkle some sesame seeds on top. We used to cut out these branches with a little knife and with a *pizzica*. A pizzica is exactly like a clothespin, only smaller, made out of copper and it has little teeth in it, so when you pinch the dough, it leaves a pattern. And these were the rametti di miele, we made *them* for Christmas. We'd prepare them a day ahead, and then just before putting them in the oven we'd take a white napkin and wet them so they'd

* The dried stalk of the giant fennel, *Ferula communis*.

come out shiny. But the quantities, how we made the dough – I don't remember any more. It was semolina flour, though, and honey.

Other things have gotten lost, too. At the San Carlo we used to make a biscuit called *biscotto al lievito*, leavened biscuit. This biscuit was shaped like a horseshoe, just like a horseshoe. We'd work it into a dough in the evening – flour, leavening, sugar, ammonium – and leave it to rise all night. Then in the morning, before we baked the biscuits, we'd knead the dough all over again, and shape the biscuits, and then we'd make all the little Easter decorations, little roses and things. And the biscuit came out white, white, white. Ever so white! And they were something to eat!

And then another thing that's gotten lost they used to make at the Convent of San Salvatore. You make it with pig's blood – *sanguinaccio*, blood pudding. But there they made the blood pudding in a special way: they mixed it with almonds, and tiny pieces of candied citron, and raisins, and cloves and cinnamon, and it made a thick paste. And then they'd make shells out of almond paste and fill them with this sanguinaccio, and the top was all embroidered with little marzipan hearts and flowers, and then they covered it with a very thin icing, chocolate, or maybe sugar. They were so beautiful! Nobody makes them any more. No more. Cloves, and cinnamon, and then if it was too liquid – it had to be a really thick paste to keep its shape – if it was too liquid you could add a little semolina flour, just a tiny bit. And when they made these things during the war, when there wasn't any marzipan, they'd put the sanguinaccio straight into serving dishes, and then it was all embroidered with *zuccata*, with little slices of zuccata.

I can remember making zuccata at the San Carlo. All that work! Zuccata is candied squash, made with those long squashes, the dark green ones? A special kind, bigger than melons. They're dark green and the flesh inside is green too; it's a special squash for making zuccata. It takes forty days to make it, maybe even longer. First you have to peel these squashes and cut them into pieces, then you salt them and put them under a weight for ten days. Then you have to take them out of the salt and soak them in water for eight days, because they've got to come sweet again. Every day you have to change the water. When all the saltiness is gone, you make a syrup: you put sugar on the squash, and when that melts, you drain it off and add more sugar to it and cook it into a syrup. If you want, you can add colouring, to make it red, or green, and then you pour it over the squash. We used to put the pieces of squash into jars, glazed earthenware jars, you know, the big tall ones that they store oil in? We'd arrange all the pieces of squash in the jars and pour the boiling syrup over them. The next day we'd drain off the syrup and boil it up again and pour it back on the squash. And so forth, day after day, until the squash was all coloured. It's so much work. Nobody does it any more. I used to, but not any more, I simply can't. But they were wonderful recipes, these ones that have disappeared.

So that's what we did for the feast days – then maybe for Saint Peter and Saint Paul we'd make a few keys, pastries in the shape of keys, always out of pasta di conserva. And then we made the mostaccioli and then biscuits, all the other biscuits: sesame *reginette* (26), milk biscuits (24), aniseed biscuits (25), *quaresimali* (29). Then the genovesi, but not very many of those. We made some almond pastries, but not

31

many; in those days, things like *belli e brutti* (8), like *sospiri* (10), like *palline* (13, 14) were made to order.

The tarts too we made on order, quince tarts or cream tarts – *crostate di marmellata* (18) or *di crema* (20) – but rarely, because back then it wasn't the custom to buy pastries for Sunday dinner. People bought pastries if they had to give someone a present, the people who came from all the farms and villages around, from Ballata, from Baida, or Dattilo. This township was one of the biggest in Sicily then, the second, I believe. Once the biggest township in Sicily was Monreale, and then came Erice, and all the taxes and the fines and everything had to be paid at Erice. People used to come up on their donkeys, by horseback, by mule.

For instance, people would come up to Erice: 'Come on, we've got to give them some pastries, let's go to the nuns' and buy a kilo of pastries.' Or else a kilo of mostaccioli, which were always welcome. Or, for instance, all the wealthy families in the Trapani area, the ones who had the big country estates, after the grape harvest they'd all come up to Erice for a while. Erice was full of people then. They would stay at Erice, and anyone who wanted to buy some of their olive oil would come to us to buy a half-kilo of mostaccioli as a present for them, and then the man who brought them vegetables would buy a quarter-kilo of mostaccioli to give to them. These were our sales. It wasn't as if there were tourists then; Erice has become famous now, but what was here before?

And then, bit by bit, the boom really started, in the Sixties. The pastry boom began and I remember once, one Sunday, it was a Sunday in August and we ran out of almond pastries at the San Carlo. So Suor Stellina said, 'We've got to make

32

some bocconcini.' So we lit the oven, the little one, not the big one. And we made some bocconcini – as many as we could, ten kilos, fifteen kilos, I forget. And since we didn't work on Sundays – it was a sin to work on Sundays – the nun had to give all the money we made from those pastries to the priest!

We'd make maybe ten or fifteen kilos of pasta di conserva a week but a lot more mostaccioli. We only made mostaccioli every other week, but enough to fill up a whole chest, maybe forty kilos, fifty kilos. Then we used to make little tiny mostaccioli with the sugar left over from the zuccata. When you make zuccata, there's all this coloured syrup left over, and we'd take this and add some more sugar and make these little mostaccioli. These sold for 300 lire a kilo, since they were a little red because of the red colouring, or maybe a little green – it was to use up these leftovers. And these little mostaccioli sold for 300 lire a kilo to the people who couldn't afford to buy the big ones. Those cost 600 a kilo; when I entered the San Carlo, the mostaccioli cost 600 lire the kilo, and the pasta di conserva and the bocconcini cost 1,200 lire. Expensive! We had to buy the almonds though, we paid 300 lire a kilo for the almonds.

The *rosolio* (37, 38, 39) were the cordials we made for weddings. Because when there was a wedding back then it wasn't as if there was a proper reception. And the poor people, the ones who couldn't afford a meal, would have rosolio and miliddi, *miliddi ri badia*, 'of the abbey', which were a sort of bread biscuit. They were like a St Martin's Day biscuit, but without any icing. We made a bread dough, flour with a little leavening and a little anise and that's all, and then shaped it into biscuits and let it rise. And they were crisp, we baked them twice, until they were very crisp. And then rosolio.

Those who had a little more money served *fantasia*. Fantasia were like the biscuits we call *te-tù*, but they were coloured green, red, or yellow, because they were made with that syrup, the coloured syrup from the zuccata. Te-tù are basically a poor man's biscuit. It's a biscuit – for instance, if you have any sugar-on-the-slab left over, if you have any left-over slices of sponge cake or any leftover tart, or some mostaccioli that got burned, you grind them all up together and make a dough out of them. See this dark colour – it's not as if that was chocolate. There's burnt mostaccioli in there, there's burnt genovesi that we couldn't sell, all that sort of thing. You knead them all together, add a little sugar, grind up an orange, or some orange peel – whatever's around – then you add a little cloves and you make these biscuits. They take a little cinnamon, and a little ammonium too. They bake in a hot oven for about ten minutes, until they are browned, and then you take them out and put them in a very, very slow oven until they dry out. It's anything that's left – recycling!

These things and then the rosolio; for example, if you had to marry off your daughter, you'd come to the nuns and say, 'Will you make me ten litres of rosolio and ten kilos of miliddi?' And these were the weddings of the ones who couldn't afford to buy a cow, the ones who didn't have the possibility of serving meat.

Or maybe they'd order some almond *torrone*, almonds in caramelized sugar, spread out on the marble to cool and then cut into pieces. The nuns made that too, but only for special occasions, not to sell every day. Or they'd make *cubbaita di giuggiulena*. The same procedure, but instead of almonds, sesame seeds, and here you have to add a little honey, to make it chewier.

And then I remember there were the *canestrini* that we made on the high feast days as gifts for the authorities, the president of the ECA, the archpriest, our confessors, our doctor, even the mayor. They were rectangles of marzipan with raised edges, like little baskets, filled with ricotta cream and all embroidered with flowers and leaves of coloured marzipan. Then they were iced like the pasta di conserva and dried in the oven. We made the baskets the day before we filled them and we put them to dry overnight, because if it's too fresh, almond paste sticks to your mouth. Sometimes after they were filled and iced and dried in the oven, we'd sprinkle on a few chocolate shavings, just a few. And these were gifts. If you didn't want to do the flowers, you could decorate them with zuccata. Most people don't even remember these things. They were very old recipes, the ones we made as gifts.

2

As I taped the first interviews with Maria, I had to watch and learn how she made her almond pastries, for *Gourmet* wanted some recipes as well. Seeing the pastries take shape at Erice, and then reproducing them in my own kitchen, I realized that these little tea cakes, the bocconcini, sospiri, and palline for which, in Sicily at least, Maria is best known, are not exactly the luxury items they appear to be as they sit in tempting heaps in her shop. None of them calls for particularly exotic ingredients: with the exception of sugar, rum, and chocolate, most of the raw materials the nuns employed were produced locally, often on the lands belonging to the institute itself. With the help of the wonderful, flavourful Sicilian almonds, which are now grown almost exclusively in the area of Avola, near Syracuse, but were once fairly common in the hills to the north of Erice, the nuns of the San Carlo were able to create considerable variety from a very limited list of ingredients and techniques.

None of their recipes calls for the more expensive pistachios, for example, which are, on the contrary, a very basic ingredient for the pastries that the nuns of the Badia dello Spirito Santo in Agrigento still produce; but then pistachios are produced in the Agrigento area, and not in the province of Trapani. Even the rum-soaked raisins that Maria puts in her *dolcetti al liquore* (9) turn out in the original version to have been locally produced Zibibbo table grapes that the nuns themselves preserved in spirits, while drying the less-than-perfect grapes on the bunch into raisins for a Carnival treat.

The frugality with which the nuns managed their culinary affairs, and which they carried to amazing extremes in what Maria aptly calls the 'recycling' of the te-tù, is rooted in the general attitude of Sicilians toward their food, an attitude in which waste has no part at all, and extravagance serves only to underline the exceptionality of the feast to be celebrated or the status to be vaunted. But it is also a direct result of the particular history of the Istituto San Carlo.

Contrary to what many people, including many of the orphans themselves, believed, the San Carlo was never a proper convent. Founded in 1617 as a shelter for nubile women of all ages, it was always a lay institution. The original endowment, a house belonging to a wealthy priest named Maranzano, was multiplied many times over by further pious bequests of property. Thanks to these donations, which often required that a part of the revenues should go to maintaining a given number of spinsters belonging to the donor's family, the San Carlo enjoyed a considerable income from its country estates and a physical plant of some fifty rooms, an assemblage of adjacent houses and churches that had been either purchased or bequeathed, and which embraced a noteworthy sampling of medieval and baroque domestic architecture.

The actual management of the institute was placed in the hands of the Tertiary Order of Franciscans, again, lay sisters who had not completed their vows, and who were often recruited from the ranks of the Sancarline, as the institute's charges became known. Local, almost personal tradition imposed the observance of certain rules proper to a cloistered order, hence the selling of pastries by wheel and grate rather than across the counter, but the so-called nuns had no formal obligation to observe these rules, and there does, in fact, seem to have been considerably more coming and going than the ex-Sancarline are apt to let on.

If in its heyday the San Carlo was very wealthy, and as a lay institution it lost nothing in the confiscation of ecclesiastical properties in the nineteenth century, nonetheless its income was slowly eroded. Most of its estates were rented out in *enfiteusi*, a perpetual contract at fixed fees that had allowed many of the vast ecclesiastical and aristocratic estates of Sicily to be brought under intensive cultivation but eventually proved ruinous to the original owners as inflation ate away at the value of their rents. By 1952, when Maria entered the San Carlo, its agricultural income would have been minimal, and the trade in pastries, paltry as it was, must have been crucial to the institute's survival.

As Maria herself says, at that time everyone in Erice was hanging on by the skin of their teeth. The Second World War left extreme indigence in its wake, there were no jobs to be had, nor had the war-damaged factories of the north yet begun to absorb the unemployed workers of the south. Even today Erice in winter seems moribund, and it is only in spring and summer, when busloads of tourists crowd the quiet streets and the empty houses fill up with vacationers seeking the cool mountain air, that Erice comes alive, a development that no-one in the impoverished 1950s could have foreseen.

The atmosphere within the San Carlo itself must have been truly funereal, with the last survivors from Erice's other convents waiting their turn to die, and no new blood coming in. Maria left sometime around 1962; in 1969 the institute was closed and the remaining orphans, all well into adulthood, were sent out into the world, leaving one solitary and aged nun and the elderly lay worker known as Suor Stellina. Without proper maintenance, the building itself began to erode, and in 1980, when Suor Maria Angela was taken to a home for the elderly in eastern Sicily, many of the rooms were declared unsafe for habitation.

The central nucleus, where the nuns and their charges spent most of their time, remains fairly intact and is often open to the public, especially in the summertime when the 'Salerniana' Cultural Association holds its annual art exhibit. I had often gone there in the early Eighties, knowing that it was a former convent, noting the double grate and the revolving iron wheel where the pastries were sold – but not realizing that the room to the right, unfurnished except for one built-in marble-topped table, was the workroom where 'sugar on a slab' had been beaten for hour after hour, or that the big room at the top of the courtyard stairs, where white-washed walls, vaulted ceilings, and sky-blue majolica tiles underfoot provide a stunning setting for contemporary paintings and sculpture, was in fact the refectory.

It wasn't until I went with Mark Ferri, the photographer sent by *Gourmet*, that I began to imagine the San Carlo as Maria knew it, with Suor Stellina sitting at the marble table and painting cheeks on the marzipan fruit, and Maria climbing up the stone stairs in the courtyard to water the vases of pansies and begonias that are still there today. Of the three courtyards, the two still accessible are small, medieval in scale, and clearly domestic in origin: the laundry room with its big stone tubs opens off one side of the inner court, and a closed door conceals the smoke-blackened room where the big wood-burning ovens are slowly collapsing. The San Carlo has the haphazard quality that comes of building by accretion, with none of the sweeping elegance that one finds in the Palermo convents founded in the seventeenth century; its inhabitants had neither time nor space for leisurely meditation.

The day began very early at the San Carlo. We woke up about six-thirty. No, earlier, about six we got up. It was still dark – so cold you could die! We got up, we washed, and we went into church to pray. The Church of San Carlo was next door. Not that we went outside to go to church; we'd go into the choir through an inner door and watch from behind the choir screen. We could see the other people because we were looking down from above, but they couldn't see us; we were always behind the screen. First we'd say our prayers, and then at seven-thirty sharp there'd be Mass. And after Mass we'd have breakfast.

The nuns made coffee in a saucepan. It's true, they cooked it in an earthenware saucepan over the coals. First they ground the coffee, coffee mixed with barley, because coffee was expensive, and then they boiled it up in the saucepan. And then they'd let it settle and that was their coffee. But the grounds that went to the bottom didn't get thrown away. The nuns added more water and brought them to a boil again, and that was *caffiata*. Coffee for the nuns and caffiata for us. And they watered the milk too. They'd give us water, caffiata, and a little bit of milk. And I used to take it and throw it down the toilet.

Everyone had a job to do: the one who was gardener went off to transplant the flowers, to water them, or whatever there was to be done; the one who was sacristan went to prepare the church; the one who was housekeeper had to carry the cheese, the pasta, the oil, and everything up to the kitchen; the one who was cook heated the milk – she lit the coals and heated the milk; and the one who was nurse had to go take care of anyone who was sick.

We had our breakfast, bread and milk, and then we'd go downstairs to the workroom, not those with special jobs but the others, to do whatever work there was to do, to make marzipan – frutta di Martorana or hearts or lambs, depending on the season. Then there was the day that we had to shell almonds, so we'd shell almonds; or the day that we had to peel almonds, so we'd peel almonds. We used a hammer and a stone to shell the almonds: eight of us working for a week could shell four *salme* of almonds – that's about 800 kilos. It takes five kilos of whole almonds to make one kilo of shelled almonds. And we didn't throw the shells away, we used them to fire the oven.

There was the day we had to make preserves, so we'd make preserves, peach preserves (34) for the tarts, or maybe citron. Conserva di cedro is really a lot of work; you can't make it any more, you can't even find the citrons. The way we used to make it, you take all the rind and the pith and you grate it on a grater, a huge grater, about seventy centimetres long, and wide too, as much as forty centimetres wide. We'd put it on the table: there was the grater part, which was metal, curved metal, and a wooden box underneath. And we'd

41

grate, two of us at a time, one on one side and one on the other. Then this grated rind was washed, tied up in a muslin bag and washed. You had to wring out all the water, then soak it in clean water for five days, fresh water every morning. After about five days you can cook it, a kilo of sugar for every kilo of fruit . . . Yes, I still make a little. Last year I made some seventy, eighty kilos. I don't know about this year. Nowadays it's hard to find the citrons, you can't even get the basic ingredients any more.

At noon on the dot we had lunch. We'd ring the bell and have lunch. At the San Carlo there were big brass mortars, with four faces engraved on the side, and when the pasta was ready they'd ring the pestle inside one of these mortars and we'd all go into the refectory. They'd lean out the courtyard window, and if the pasta was boiling in the pot, 'Ting-a-ling-a-ling'. If the pasta was on the table, 'Ting-a-ling-a-ling! Ting-a-ling-a-ling!' That meant the pasta was already on the table. So everybody ran. This was our dinner bell. The pasta we ate with beans, with cauliflower, with potatoes. Monday, beans; Tuesday, cauliflower; Wednesday, favas or lentils; Thursday, *pasta asciutta*, with tomato sauce or with garlic. Friday, pasta with greens, because we had to fast on Fridays. Saturday, pasta with favas, or with potatoes. Sundays in meat broth. The ECA gave us the meat. And then we'd start all over again. It was always like that.

And in the evening too. It wasn't as if we cooked supper, as if they gave us anything to eat in the evenings. You had to save something from what they gave you at noon. If they made pasta with cauliflower, for instance, the cauliflower was the second course; each of us got a plate of pasta and a little pot with the cauliflower. And you had to save some of

42

this cauliflower for supper – if you wanted to. If not, down the toilet. I threw a lot of stuff down the toilet! Yes, we had bread too; they gave us each half a kilo of bread every morning, and we had to divide it up for the day.

And then the ones who were on kitchen duty had to wash the dishes. The others all went into the church to pray. Then we'd all go back to work, to whatever it was that we'd been doing. To the workrooms, or to shell almonds, whatever. Around about six-thirty, we had to wash our hands and go into the church for vespers, and then into the refectory to eat whatever we'd saved. If we'd saved anything. If not, nothing. About eight o'clock we'd go back into church to say our rosaries, and then to bed.

Free time? Never. Things to read? Noooo! We had our rosaries, church – oh, there were our missals, but it was boring always reading the same thing. And that was that. If we ever found a free moment, my sister Angela and I, we'd start playing. And when we started to fool around in church we'd get scolded. At Easter we had spiritual exercises, and on Good Friday we fasted. On Good Fridays you had to fast. And what did we care about fasting? Every Friday in Lent we had to fast, which meant that we ate only at noon, and that was that. No breakfast and no supper. You didn't eat, you fasted. At noon they made pasta cooked in milk, and I used to take it and throw it down the toilet! Cooked in milk because otherwise, since we couldn't have breakfast, they'd have had to throw the milk out. So they boiled it up with some water and cooked the pasta in it.

Once – it must have been a couple of years ago – I came home and I was wondering what to have for supper, and I thought, 'I want to make pasta in milk!' But it stank so as

43

soon as I started cooking it that I couldn't eat it. Pasta in milk: if you wanted to eat, you ate that, otherwise you fasted.

Every week we had to make our confession. Every Saturday. I never wanted to go make my confession. I used to say to the confessor, 'I haven't anything to confess, and that's that!' They were Capuchin friars. One would come every Saturday to hear our confessions and he'd ring the bell. One of us went in as the other came out. They'd ring a bell and when we heard it . . . for instance, I had a stroke, a ring, and a stroke. That's how they called me. Ninetta had four strokes, one, two, three, and four. Titì had three rings: 'Ding-a-ling, ding-a-ling, ding-a-ling'. And wherever she was, she knew that they were calling her and that she had to go and confess.

Anyone who didn't want to go to confession was sent to the middle of the refectory as punishment, and you had to kneel in front of everybody without eating. If you didn't want to go, or if, for instance, you said, 'I didn't hear any bell, I didn't know I was supposed to go to confession' – I did that a lot. But if I did right or I did wrong, I don't know. And I'm not going to worry about it.

As soon as we got to the table, Ministra would stand up and say, 'Maria, on your knees in the middle of the refectory. And the rest of us shall eat.' In the middle of the refectory! And when everybody else had finished eating: 'Now you can get up.' Your food was waiting for you. If you wanted, you could eat; if you didn't, you threw it down the toilet.

The turns for the important jobs lasted for two years. If you were *portiera*, for example, you did it for two years. Not us little ones, though, it was the big girls that had that job, because it carried a lot of responsibility, it was an important

44

job. '*She* was the portiera!' we used to say. The portiera was the one who answered the bell, the portiera was the one who sent the Auntie to do errands, the portiera was the one who sold the pastries. And then every time we baked pastries, for example, if some of the mostaccioli got burnt and couldn't be sold, the next day it was the portiera who divided them up. We'd each get a mostacciolo, or if the bocconcini got burnt, we'd each get a bocconcino; if the biscuits got burnt we'd each get a biscuit. These were the sweets that we got, the burnt ones. I used to save mine, I'd save them for my mother to give to the little ones.

Once, I remember, it was Titì who was the portiera. We had made milk biscuits. Now I really like milk biscuits, so I said – we were in the workroom where there were these great wooden chests full of biscuits, and we were making pasta di conserva – I said to the nun, 'May I have a biscuit?' And she pretended not to hear me. So I went to the chest and I took a biscuit. Titì made me put it back. I felt so awful. I didn't say anything. I went into the bathroom and I started to cry. I had a good cry over that biscuit. And then I said, 'Why do I have to cry about this? No biscuits. That's that.'

With these important jobs you changed every two years, but with the kitchen it was every two weeks. Two weeks one girl and two weeks another. A big one and a little one, always, to do the cooking. For example, when we finished supper and came out of church on Friday evenings, Ministra used to say, 'Maria and Ninetta tomorrow go on kitchen duty.' Because the turn ended on Friday. You cleaned the kitchen on Friday and turned it over to the next girls: 'Maria and Ninetta take over the kitchen.' Or maybe: 'Maria and 'Nofria on kitchen duty!'

We did the cooking on a wood stove, a big girl and a little one, we did the cooking for everyone. Once, I remember, I was on kitchen duty with Ninetta, and she went off and left me to fry – I wonder where she went, to confession maybe? Anyway, she left me to fry at least five kilos of *baccalà*. And I was only eleven, I'd never fried any baccalà. Over the coals! As she went out she said to me, 'My friend, you've got to fry this baccalà.' So I set to work to fry the baccalà. But with baccalà you can't turn it over until it's browned on the bottom, or it will all fall apart. And that baccalà surely did fall apart. Then she came back and said, 'What have you done?' Had I ever fried before? She could have told me, if she'd been smart she could have said that you have to brown it first. Not like that!

Then at the end of two weeks you gave the kitchen a good cleaning, and another shift took over. They always used to make us little girls be the gardeners, together with a big girl. In the spring you had to take out all the flowers and put them in new pots, water them every evening, everything like that. It was nice, though, when a new flower came up while you were gardener and you'd say to yourself, '*Madonna mia*, look, a new flower!' Then there was the nursing, that lasted two years too. If somebody was sick, you took care of them, there was medicine to give, the old nuns to take care of. They always used to make me be the nurse and cope with the old nuns, wash them when they died. I washed my first dead person when I was thirteen.

Then once a week we had to do the laundry. At the San Carlo we had to wash our personal laundry ourselves, and Suor Stellina did everything else. But our handkerchiefs we washed ourselves, and our underpants, our stockings, even our sanitary napkins. Suor Stellina would put them in to soak in *lemmuni*. In lemmuni, big earthenware basins glazed green on the inside. She'd put our laundry in to soak and we'd wash it. And I remember how Suor Stellina used to put her hands over my hands, and teach me to wash, to scrub. There was a laundry room with five big stone washtubs in it, great big ones. And we had to scrub things on these great stone washboards, you can imagine what it was like. You had to scrub until you raised blisters on your hands. With liquid soap and leached *liscivia*, lye made from ashes, olive wood ashes. The best lye comes from olive wood.

When we washed down in the laundry tubs, first we used the lye and then the *cuffino*. Cuffino. To make the laundry smell nice. We boiled up water and bay leaves, then we'd filter it and pour it over the laundry, and let it stand a night, so everything smelled of bay. Then the next day we'd wring it out and hang it up to dry.

First of all came the *nitiata*: you put the laundry in to soak in hot water and soap. The nitiata. Then you'd scrub it, wring it out, and put it in hot water again, this time with both soap and lye, and you'd scrub it some more. That was the first *lisciata*. Then came the second lisciata, with just lye, still scrubbing. Then came the first *pilata*, the rinsing, and then the second pilata and then the cuffino, and then the next day you'd hang it out. There was a cistern in the room where the washtubs were, a huge cistern, and we'd bring up water with a bucket. There are a lot of cisterns in the San Carlo: one in the laundry room, one in the workroom; in the courtyard, there's another; in the parlatory, there's another; still another in the kitchen, all filled with rainwater. All the water that we needed for the pastries, for washing, for cleaning, was all pulled up by hand with buckets. Hand over hand; we didn't have a pulley. When we did the wash in the laundry room, that's how we filled all those tubs.

We each had our turn: for instance, Tuesdays it would be your turn and Wednesdays it was mine. Each of us little ones was entrusted to a bigger girl, and she was in charge of us. So when it was her turn to do laundry, we'd go too, we'd stand next to her and do our laundry, learn how to wash. She would help us wash our personal things, and when we were still little she would wash our sheets for us, but we'd help. And that was when Ninetta used to play tricks on me, she used to say to me, 'My friend, scrub these dish towels for me.' She'd put her sanitary napkins in to soak, and when the stains were gone, she'd call me: 'Come here, my dear, come and scrub these towels for me.' And I, like a fool, would go and scrub these . . . these 'towels'. I really thought they were towels.

How I used to scrub. She always used to say to me, 'When you scrub, your hands have got to have play, you mustn't do it like that, with your fists closed tight.' Ooooh! Those 'towels' got a good scrubbing. And then she used to make me shine her shoes. And I'd do it. But once she told my sister, 'Shine my shoes!' And my sister Angela, younger than me she was, took the shoe polish and spread it all over the insides of the shoes. Ninetta never asked her again.

Angela was a devil. She was the youngest of all. Instead I had to act like a big girl, for my sake and for hers, for my mother used to tell me, 'Be careful, my child, be careful about this, be careful about that!'

I laugh about these things now with Ninetta, but I was happy to do them for her. Whatever she did to me, whatever

48

she said, I never took it badly . . . no, no. Only with Titì. I couldn't stand Titì.

And yet, when it was time to do the laundry, I was always the first in line, anything not to have to scrub the stairs. All the stairs in the San Carlo were stone, inside and out. After you went over them with soap and brush, you had to go back over them again with a pumice stone. You had to scrub each step with pumice stone until it turned white. And you can imagine what it was like, rubbing stone on stone . . .

And then, when it was time to use the oven, to light the oven, we did that in turns, too, two by two. Let's say, for instance, that tomorrow is baking day, right? And it's our turn, yours and mine. At one o'clock in the morning we'd have to get up, to go and light the fire. They'd come and knock at one, and we'd get up – I hated it! It was cold enough to die in those old buildings. You had to light the fire because by four o'clock, when the nuns came – they would get up about four – the oven had to be ready, so that we could begin to bake the mostaccioli, the biscuits, whatever needed baking.

A brick oven has to heat up really well, it has to turn white. The dome above, we call it the *cielo*, the heaven, is ready as soon as it turns white. You can also tell by rubbing a stick of ferla on the floor; if sparks fly when you rub the ferla over the bricks, then it's ready. We had two ovens in the bakery, a great big one that held forty pans, each forty by sixty centimetres, and then a little one. Sometimes we needed a sponge cake in a hurry, or a tart, and so in order not to fire that great big oven, we'd use the little one.

At one a.m. we'd light the fire. The first batch would go in about six, in wintertime. Because it took all that time for the oven to heat up, to turn white. It took that long. We'd make mostaccioli first, about five or six batches. Each batch of mostaccioli called for twenty *rotoli* of flour, nine rotoli of sugar . . .

Rotoli. A rotolo is 800 grammes. All the measures for the mostaccioli, for the bocconcini, and so on, everything was measured in rotolos, and then there was the *oncia, oncias* and half-*oncias*. We didn't use kilos. The bocconcini recipe was in rotolos: it called for a rotolo of almonds and half a rotolo plus an oncia and a half of preserves. When I came out of the San Carlo, I had to convert all the measurements, because the young girls no longer understood these things. I could understand them, but who else could? So from then on I did everything in kilos. It was a bit difficult for me at the beginning because I wasn't used to them. Also because at the San Carlo we didn't have proper weights. We had scales, you know, the kind with two brass plates that balance, and as weights we used pebbles and cobblestones, with the weight written on, like one rotolo, or one half-rotolo, or one oncia – an oncia was sixty grammes, it was. What kind of weights do you use in America?

After the mostaccioli we baked the milk biscuits, some fifteen kilos or so, then two batches of bocconcini, then we did the icing on the pasta di conserva. Then at the end, when the oven was barely warm, we baked the amaretti. I put in a long apprenticeship at the San Carlo: for the first three years I did nothing but scrape the pans. They had to be perfectly clean; if I made a mistake I got a rap on the knuckles.

There was a little door in the room where the ovens were, a door that gave onto the Via San Carlo. We used it to put out the garbage, or when the firewood was delivered. And when we were on the same shift with Ninetta, my sister and

I, when she had to open that door, we'd use it to escape. We'd beg and beg and Ninetta would say, 'Come back immediately.' She'd spit on the step and say, 'See that? You have to be back before that dries!' And we'd race down the street and run around the square like crazy and race back again. Sometimes there were puppet shows in the square and we would watch for a minute. Those were our escapes.

Oven duty lasted until about eleven o'clock at night. Twenty-two hours! When there was smoke, our eyes would get so red. Then you had to go and wash up, so whoever had been on kitchen duty filled up a big kettle, but it was cold. You had to wash yourself with cold water, since we didn't have any gas. So sometimes, do you know what I'd do? I'd take the kettle and stick it in the oven. How could you wash yourself with ice water?

And that was the day at the San Carlo.

We didn't make our bread ourselves, it came from the outside, store-bought, at least from the time I was there. They used to give us pasta and half a kilo each of bread a day. The ECA provided it from the convent lands, with the wheat from the holdings, and then a quarter of a litre of milk from those who pastured their cows on these holdings. These people brought their milk to Erice, and they had to take turns, a month at a time, to deliver five or six litres every day, according to how many we were, a quarter of a litre each. Then they gave us meat on Sundays, and firewood, and cheese – the people who used our pastures sent cheese – and then olive oil. All this the ECA gave us from the lands belonging to the San Carlo. Plus the ECA provided 30,000 lire a month; the bookkeeper came to see Ministra at the end of each month, and gave her 30,000 lire for daily expenses. She used it to pay the light bill, for example, and for us little ones who didn't have anything when we came, she had to buy mattresses and bedsprings, she had to provide blankets, our uniforms, underwear and stuff.

When we girls entered the San Carlo, Suor Stellina sewed a wardrobe for us; the ECA purchased all the material, and Suor Stellina sewed everything, our underpants, nightgowns, all that. But we didn't have underpants like you do today, cut way high up on the thigh, because we weren't supposed to have all that skin showing. And you couldn't walk around without an undershirt there, not even in the summertime when you were on oven duty. Not even in your own room – no walking around in a petticoat without an undershirt! First thing in the morning you had to put on an undershirt. Long sleeves in the winter and short sleeves in the summer, ready-made. Our stockings were made for us, though; there was a woman here in Erice, the sister of one of the nuns, Angela la Calzatara – the 'Stocking Maker' – who knitted them on a machine, cotton stockings or wool ones. Black! Gorgeous! Weren't they just!

It wasn't as if there were nylon stockings in those days, just cotton or wool ones. And when we were a little older, when I was about eighteen or nineteen, we washed these stockings so often that they faded, they turned white at the heels, and we thought it looked ugly. So when we had to go out, me, Titì, and so on, we didn't want to go out like that, and silly girls that we were, we used to rub them with shoe polish where they had faded. We made a terrible mess. But those faded stockings, we just couldn't stand those faded stockings.

Once the girls who were bigger than me wanted to use

bras, and the nuns said, 'Girls! For shame!' Such things were unheard of. Nobody ever wore a bra in the San Carlo. Nobody ever had store-bought underpants, never! Home-sewn underpants with long, loose thighs. They tried to teach me to sew them. 'You must learn to do the backstitch,' they'd say.

We had uniforms for going out, for processions: dark blue dresses with white collars, and jackets over them. For inside the convent, whatever we had: a smock, a hand-me-down from one of the bigger girls, a dress that didn't fit her any more. Or, for instance, people would give old sweaters and things to the nuns, who would divide them up: 'This would fit you, this would fit you, that would fit you.' Then they bought us our shoes, and that was that. Oh, and we had capes, blue wool capes for the winter, no coats. Some of the bigger girls who had money had coats made for themselves, but they had to be blue. We little ones had the capes that the ECA gave us. Dark blue, always. Black stockings, cotton in summer, woollen in winter. Black shoes, and that was that. Petticoats: you were in trouble if you didn't wear a petticoat, a flannel petticoat. Then there were our nightgowns and the sheets, two pairs of sheets, one on and one off. If we tore something, we had to mend it ourselves. There was mending day, and we'd sit round Suor Stellina and mend all our things, put everything in order. And that was the wardrobe at the San Carlo.

But for accompanying the dead we had black dresses. For accompanying the dead. When someone died, a coffin to accompany, we went out – I couldn't bear it. We orphans had to go and accompany the coffin, black dresses, black stock-ings, and a black veil on our heads, one of those black tulle veils, you know, the ones you tie under your chin like a kerchief? I hated them. I won't wear anything black. Maybe a skirt, but nothing else. Black underwear, a black petticoat, no, nothing! I hate black!

We had to go to the church for the funeral, and then when they left the church we would walk in front of the coffin. Two by two we walked, the little ones in front and the big girls behind. A nun in front and one at the back. And we had to say our rosaries, all the way to the cemetery, 'Ma-RU-ru-ru-ru, rah-RU-ru-ru-ru'. And if you didn't, the nun was there: 'So why aren't you praying?' That's what she'd say, 'Why aren't you praying?' and give a good pull on your braids. And at the end, at the cemetery, the nun would pay her condolences and the family would make an offering for the orphan girls. Money. I couldn't stand it, ever. Maybe it's the saddest thing that I can remember, this walking in the funeral processions. And what did we care? I mean, I was sorry that the person had died and all that, but what did it matter to me? All dressed up in uniform, black uniforms with white collars for accompanying the dead.

The Erice cemetery is halfway down the mountainside, where there's the chapel. There's a beautiful painting in that chapel, the *Madonna della Confusione*; it feels like the eyes are speaking to you. Maybe I liked it because it's a person's eyes that attract me. In that picture of the Madonna, the eyes seemed to be speaking to me. The *Madonna della Confusione*. They say that if you get in a muddle, you're supposed to pray to this Madonna and she'll help you.

When we got to the chapel, the monks were there to bless the coffin. We girls would have to go into the chapel to say our prayers and then we'd walk back up to Erice again.

Accompanying the dead took at least an hour and a half, maybe more. We had to walk slowly. On the way back we'd take shortcuts, but we had to keep quiet, we had the nun with us. 'Girls! What is this laughter? We've been to a funeral! We're coming from a funeral!' Actually, I never take that road any more if I can help it.

What did we care, at that age? Somebody would come on behalf of the family, they'd bring flowers, for example, they'd bring us pasta, or they'd bring us meat. For me it was . . . I don't know. It was humiliating. Or they'd send an envelope. These big important men, big daddies, supermen, very pious, they'd die, and leave an offering for the nuns – who knows what sins they had to be forgiven for!

We wore black on Good Friday, too, for the procession, for the Mysteries and Our Lady of Sorrows. Black dresses and black veils, because we were in mourning. On Good Friday we had to keep the veils on all day, because of being in mourning. I've always hated these veils, ever since my father died and I had to wear black stockings and a black veil. I hate black, that's all there is to it.

I remember when my father died, we all had to wear black: me and my sister, who was only six, all dressed in black, black stockings, a black cotton kerchief all the time, and a long black veil over that when we went out. My brother Nardo, smaller than I was, with a black beret, a black ribbon on his sleeve, and black buttons . . .

Such things aren't human. But they happened. They were allowed to happen. When my mother died – I was very attached to my mother, but when she died I didn't wear black. It wasn't because I didn't love her, I felt terrible. But that I should do something just for appearance's sake, no, never.

'We wore black on Good Friday, too, for the procession . . . Black dresses and black veils.' The girls with veils are Angela and Ninetta (*front, left to right*) and Maria and Titì with Suor Teresa behind.

Maria is well aware that she is heir to an ancient tradition, nothing of which had ever been consigned to paper, and no sooner had the article been published than she began to urge that we do a book together, to preserve for posterity all the recipes that she had learned at the San Carlo. But I had other projects underway, so I said no. It was on a short trip we made together that I changed my mind.

Maria had been invited to Regaleali, the big wine-producing estate in the centre of Sicily that belongs to Count Giuseppe Tasca. The count's eldest daughter, the Marchesa Anna Tasca Lanza, organizes cooking courses there, and had asked Maria if she would be willing to come and demonstrate how she makes frutta di Martorana. I was to accompany her.

It was a very successful day. Maria immediately gained the sympathy of Mario, the Tasca chef who conceals behind his cheerful, easygoing manner a certain reluctance to share the limelight. 'Cheffie', she called him, and he loved it. Everyone was gripped by the seemingly absent-minded dexterity with which she could transform, almost without looking, a lump of almond paste into a perfectly formed apricot. And although I had often gone to restaurants with Maria and had noted how much she enjoyed being the successful business-woman taking the American journalist out to lunch, I was unprepared for the perfect poise with which she navigated in what was a warm, welcoming, but potentially intimidating setting.

The trip home began in silence. As I drove I was wondering what it was in Maria's background that had given her the strength not only to survive, but to triumph. It was not my still unsatisfied curiosity, however, that sealed our literary partnership, but Maria's musings, of a very different nature than mine. She began thinking out loud about the lunch we had just eaten, for which two Neapolitan chefs taking the course had prepared an unusual and delicious dish of pork innards cooked in tomato sauce. It reminded her of something from her childhood, and suddenly as she talked I understood the extent of the riches I would squander if I were to neglect the opportunity she was offering me.

They used to make a dish like that for weddings, old-fashioned weddings, the kind they used to have out in the country. Once I got permission to leave the San Carlo for one of these weddings, it was the wedding of a cousin. Not the one that got married right after my father died – that wedding we could only watch from the window because we were in mourning. I cried and cried, I could have killed myself, I wanted to go so much. But when you were in mourning, you couldn't go out. All shut in with the shutters closed! I remember that there was a crack in one of the shutters and us kids peeking through the crack because we wanted to see the bride. My father had only been dead three months and we had to stay with the shutters closed. Closed tight! And afterwards they sent us some of the food.

But the weddings that I'm talking about, the old-fashioned country weddings, they were for my cousin Pinuzza and my cousin Nutta, Uncle Michele's daughters. Country weddings were always a big feast: they would slaughter a beast, one calf, two calves, depending on the number of guests. There was a cook who used to go and cook at these weddings, he'd bring the plates and the pots and forks and knives, and move in a couple of days ahead of time. He cut up the meat and stewed it, boiled veal and raw celery, I remember, and bread. This is what you'd eat for dinner, about two o'clock or so.

Then towards midnight you'd eat again. The poorer people would serve celery again, raw celery and pieces of cheese, but the ones who were rich enough would serve the veal innards, cooked in a way that we used to call *antipasto*. In a sweet-and-sour sauce – delicious! To make antipasto, first you have to boil the innards, and then you make a sauté of garlic, onions, and celery – and those who could afford it would add olives and capers – it all depended. Then salt and pepper and tomato sauce. After it had cooked a little, you put in the innards, and then you added a bit of sugar, and when it was time to take it off the fire, you added vinegar. Sweet and sour.

We used to have antipasto at the San Carlo as well. Every so often Ciccio Italiano the Butcher would make us a present of some innards on a feast day. And when the nuns made it, after they put it in the serving dish they'd sprinkle it with toasted almonds. It was wonderful!

So that was a country wedding: there was dancing and music, someone would play an accordion, or maybe an ocarina. And at the end we would accompany the bride and groom to their new house, with the music. They'd go in the door and shut it behind them, and they wouldn't come out for a week. Then on the eighth day the bride would get all dressed up and they'd go and pay calls on the people who had come to the wedding. They were something, those weddings! I remember that when Uncle Michele's Pinuzza got married, my brother Nardo almost lost his toenails, he was on his feet so long, serving at table and dancing. As far as I can remember, I was still at the San Carlo when Pinuzza got married. When her sister Nutta got married, I had already left, and that must have been the last country wedding to be held in this area.

3

New taping sessions were in order. I would make the hour's drive from my farm to Erice in the morning and spend the day in the back room of the pastry shop, a long, narrow kitchen with the tiered electric ovens at one end, a large steel refrigerator at the other, and grinding and mixing machines crowding along the walls. Wheeled iron racks, six feet tall, hold trays of genovesi and almond cakes, pallid as they await their turn in the oven, or golden and fragrant as they cool. In the middle stands a long and narrow marble-topped table, where endless quantities of almond paste and pasta frolla are rolled out, shaped, filled, moulded, and painted, a little dough at a time, using miniature rolling pins no more than ten inches long so that as many as six people can work at once without bumping into each other.

The number varies according to the demand for pastries: Maria and her brother Nardo are always present; her nieces Antonina and Lella show up when business is good; and at the peak there may be two or three seasonal workers as well, rolling almond balls between the palms of their hands or cutting out domed genovesi with a scalloped cookie cutter. It's never a quiet spot: the owner of a café in a neighbouring town rings up to order the week's supply of almond pastries;

Nardo staggers in with a fifty-pound sack of blanched almonds on his shoulder and empties it resoundingly into a big steel bin; clients call out from the front in a variety of accents and languages, or – if they are local people – pull a chair up to the worktable and join in the conversation.

With pen and notebook to back up the tape recorder – *tuo aggeggio*, Maria calls it, 'your gadget' – the kitchen is the best place to get Maria's recipes. She can reach for a hunk of marzipan in order to demonstrate the shape of a *barchetta di sanguinaccio* or jump up to show me some unfamiliar ingredient such as 'sugar on a slab', and, for lack of a written record, she can consult Nardo's or Lella's memory when hers fails. Which is not often – I am constantly amazed at how she can mention a dish she hasn't thought about for years, and then tell me exactly how many grammes of each ingredient are required. Of course, Maria's 'exactly' is that of any great cook: her recipes change with her mood and the weather, and I find comfort in her co-workers who are somewhat less self-assured and nonchalant than she is. Then there is the problem of quantity. Most of Maria's recipes start out, 'Take fifteen kilos of almonds and thirty egg whites . . .'

Even the higher mathematics that such quantities require are possible in the confusion of the kitchen, but I want the memories as well, and I know from past experience that as soon as Maria begins to speak of events that have emotional significance for her, her voice will drop a register, the refrigerator will turn itself on, and I will be left with half of a story and a lot of hum and buzz. So I come to stay, days in the workroom, evenings as a guest in her apartment. We eat an early supper, put up our feet, and, with wine glasses to hand

and my 'gadget' propped up on the sofa between us, talk our
way into the nights.

We have chosen late January for these sessions, the lull that
comes after Christmas, and before the spring crescendo that
starts with *cannoli* for Carnival and moves on through
paschal lambs to the tourist season. Maria's professional life
is still dominated by the liturgical calendar just as it was when
she was at the San Carlo, where the only thing that distin-
guished one week from another was the nature of the task:
hearts for Christmas, lambs at Easter – a childhood spent
making sweets for other people's celebrations.

Christmas for us? We ate boiled cauliflower and fried
baccalà, you know, salt codfish. On Christmas Eve we had
fried baccalà and sometimes we made *sfinci* (45) too,
Christmas fritters. Sfinci, or a little bit of cubaita di giuggiulena for Christmas Eve. And then, after supper, we had
this Baby Jesus, this wax baby under a crystal bell, which
made the rounds of all of us. For instance, if there were
twenty of us, then we'd start twenty days before Christmas,
and one night it would be in the room where you slept and
the next night it would be in the room where I slept. And
everyone would come in, all the nuns and all the girls, and
we said our prayers in front of the Baby Jesus.

On Christmas Eve this Baby Jesus was in the Mother
Superior's room, and she'd pass around nuts and tangerines.
The ECA would send us chestnuts, the dried ones that are
still soft inside, and hazelnuts, walnuts, and tangerines. And
after prayers that evening Ministra would give them to us,

but it was the ECA that paid for them. This was our Christmas Eve.

On Christmas Day we ate fish couscous, the ECA bought us fish. We had the couscous first, and then the fish for a second course, and then if there were any tangerines left over, or any nuts, they'd give us those, and they'd make us a tart, filled either with homemade jam or with pastry cream. Or if they didn't make a tart they brought out plates of pastry cream. They'd put the cream in serving dishes and decorate it with zuccata, and we girls would divide this cream. This was our Christmas.

But on Carnival we ate meat. For Carnival we had boiled meat on Sunday, and couscous on Monday, but made with meat this time. And on Shrove Tuesday we had ragout of *polpette dolci* (46), sweet meatballs cooked in a sauce made with tomato extract. At Erice we used to make them for the Feast of the Immaculate Conception, and then for Carnival too. And, in fact, I really love them. We'd mix them up in a *madia*, a big wooden tub, because there were so many of us, and we had to put in a lot of breadcrumbs: at San Carlo we used five kilos of meat, and for that much meat you need at least three, three and a half kilos of white breadcrumbs and a kilo of grated cheese. Then we added sugar, and cinnamon, and toasted almonds, at least 200 grammes of almonds for every kilo of meat. We'd knead all this together with eggs, and shape it into meatballs, brown them in oil, and then put them in the sauce to simmer. And this was our ragout. They were so good. I haven't eaten any since. Blanched almonds – we would toast the almonds and then grind them. But those polpette, you just couldn't get enough of them! Maybe because meat used to have more taste, I don't know. But they surely were good. For Carnival we ate all this meat, and that was that. It was because the ECA sent it to us.

During Lent we didn't eat any meat at all, forty days and no meat. We ate beans and vegetables . . . beans, vegetables, and fish on Sundays. And that was that. Or sometimes on Sunday they made egg ragout or, to save money, they made *fruscidde di ova* and cooked them in the tomato sauce. Fruscidde are fritters: you take breadcrumbs and cheese – we had cheese, the ECA sent it – breadcrumbs, cheese, and you mix them with eggs and make these little egg fritters. Add a clove of garlic, add a pinch of sugar, a little cinnamon, and some parsley chopped very fine, and make it into fritters. Then you brown them and you put them in the sauce. These were the fruscidde di ova. Or you can break the eggs in the frying pan, fry them a little first on one side, then on the other, and then put them in the sauce. This is egg ragout.

For Easter we got to eat lamb; they'd send a lamb from the convent pastures, and Ciccio Italiano the Butcher would come and slaughter it for us. Then we would cook it up for Easter lunch, but always in a ragout, on account of the pasta. And we'd add a few potatoes to the sauce to make it go farther. We had lamb, and that was that. We didn't always get dessert. It depended. If Easter had gone well, if we'd sold a lot, then we made a cassata: sponge cake with preserves in the middle and decorated on top with zuccata. We made this cassata and for us it was a real treat! And we got to eat the lamb, after forty days of no meat.

Then there were two other feast days that I remember: for Ferragosto we got an ice cream and for us girls that *was* a feast. Once a year an ice cream. The Auntie went and changed her clothes and then she went and bought an ice cream cone for each of us and she brought them back. And then there was the Madonna of Custonaci, she's the patron saint of Erice and her feast day comes on the last Wednesday of August. They bought us a pizza. A real proper pizza, we looked forward to it like I don't know what! I love pizzas. I waited for that day . . . And that's all, I don't remember any other feast days. This is what they gave us. An ice cream for Ferragosto and a pizza for the Madonna.

Easter at my house? At home we usually ate *cassatedde* for Easter; at my house, my mother's house, we ate *cassatedde con la ricotta bollite*. These were a sort of ravioli, pasta turnovers filled with ricotta that had onion in it, chopped very, very fine, and parsley, pepper, salt – at my house, when I was little, as far as I can remember. We had cows, we had sheep. Ricotta, cheese, this sort of thing we had – we didn't have other, more essential things, maybe – but these we did have.

I don't remember very much from when I was little. I had only one thing to play with then, we had this little mare. If you could see Ballata where I grew up, a *baglio*, a farmhouse, and that's all. Nothing else. But how I loved the ricotta, the cheese, the animals! We used to have a cow, her name was Sciaquatedda. She gave thirty litres of milk a day. And there was a boy who looked after the sheep and the cows. His name was Nino, he's still alive today. They were the owner's cows, but we took care of them, there was a stable there. And we used to say to him, 'Nino, be careful to close the stable door when you go out!' The cows weren't supposed to be loose, they were kept inside and fed on hay and fava beans, to make them give more milk. And little me, real tiny, where was I? Under the thighs of the cow with her udder in my mouth! And the cow nursed me, the cow would give me her milk. I sucked and the cow gave me her milk! 'Where's Maria? Where's the little one? Where's the little one?' Where was the little one? Under the cow!

We owned only a little bit of land of our own. The baglio and the land that my father farmed and all the animals belonged to someone else; we were sharecroppers. But we had a little piece of land of our own – we still have it, a place called Carnevale – that my father bought when he was still a bachelor, he paid 2,300 lire for it! He bought it at an auction. There are 6,000 square metres of land, and a house that's 180 square metres, and two wells, and in front of the door there was a big mulberry tree: all summer long my brother Nardo used to sleep outside under this mulberry tree together with my father.

But we only went to stay at Carnevale in 1949. Before that we lived at Ballata, in the baglio, the Baglio Pellegrino. In the baglio itself there were us and another family, the Pellegrinos, Mario Pellegrino was the father's name. In the baglio itself. But not far away, about two or three hundred metres away, there were my grandfather, my grandmother, Uncle Carlo, Uncle Michele, then a little farther off lived Uncle Cristoforo, and then down a ways Uncle Vito. Only the women had gone away, when they got married, Aunt Peppina to Ummeri and Aunt 'Unta to Chiesanuova. He had four sons, my grandfather did, and two daughters.

Maria doesn't live up 'al monte', as the Ericini say: in 1977 she married Francesco Candela, a retired waiter considerably older than she, whose poor health required that they move down to the milder climate of Valderice. Some years after Francesco's death in 1985, she bought the apartment in which we are sitting. It is a large and very modern apartment on the upper floor of a two-storey building on the outskirts of Trapani. The downstairs houses a small biscuit factory where Maria hopes eventually, if and when she can find a competent manager, to produce marzipan and almond pastries for export.

For our evenings, we shun the large and rather formal living room with its brocade divans and antique cabinets for the cosier sitting room where Maria spends most of what little time she has at home. It is hard for me, seeing her in this setting with television, central heating, and all the other modern comforts, to imagine her in the baglio. So one day we close up the shop early, right after lunch, and Maria, Nardo, and Nardo's wife, Michela, squeeze themselves into my little Renault, which rides high over the bumpy country roads that take us to Ballata. Maria has agreed to show me the Baglio Pellegrino, and she is thrilled to be seeing it herself for the first time in over twenty years.

Nardo directs me down the mountain and across gentle hills just turning green with fava beans and winter wheat, or dark brown in fallow expectation of summer's melon crop. We roll eastwards, along roads that become narrower and narrower and eventually peter out into a dirt track. The driveway where we park leads to an isolated summer house belonging to people from the city: it is a recent structure, built on the remains of the little baglio where Uncle Vito lived.

This is as close as we can get by car. The road doesn't go as far as the Baglio Pellegrino, which stands halfway up the next hill over. The grandfather's house was on the top of the hill, but there is nothing left of that, not even a foundation, to mar the neat rows of fava plants and the lush profusion of clover and wild mustard. We cut across the hillside, following the edge of a wheat field, stepping with care to avoid trampling the tender green spears, trying not to sink ankle deep into the soft loam. Although there are rain clouds on the horizon, the windswept fields are dry underfoot. One good storm would turn this all to mud.

The baglio is the typical rural construction dotting the hills of westernmost Sicily. It would be more proper perhaps to use the dialect term, *bagghiu*, because only in Sicilian does this word, probably derived from the Spanish *patio*, mean 'courtyard', and, by extension, a group of one- or two-storey houses built around a central court. There are baglios of all sizes, some very big indeed, and I had imagined Maria's childhood home as almost a little hamlet, with lots of families grouped around a space nearly as big as a village green. I am surprised by the loneliness and the desolation of the half-ruined house: bare stone walls and sagging tiled roof, four rooms in a row giving onto a sort of terrace that is open on two sides. There is a kitchen, a bedroom, a storeroom, and a stable, but nowadays sheep have taken over everywhere, and from behind the door to the bedroom, falling off its hinges but barricaded closed, we can hear a lamb bleating.

On the other side of the wall that closes one end of the terrace there is another group of buildings and another little courtyard where the Pellegrino family lived. And still does, it turns out: a couple of elderly men have seen us wandering around and are hurrying down the hillside towards the house. Maria is terribly pleased to see these ghosts from her childhood: they are the Pellegrino brothers, hermits, she says. In their eighties and never married, they have lived out here all of their lives.

Hermits they may be, but they are delighted to have someone new to talk to, and to show us through their rooms, bare but clean-swept, the blankets neatly folded on the cots and all the ancient farming implements cared for and hung in their proper places. While Michela gathers wild mustard greens, and I stand shivering in the icy wind, Nardo and Maria and the Pellegrino brothers discuss the changes that have taken place, who has died, what houses have collapsed or been abandoned, which fields have changed hands. A piece of land that borders on theirs is up for sale, and one of the brothers says he wants to buy it. Nardo, a very practical man, asks the would-be buyer, in his eighties and without heirs, what ever he wants it for: 'For turning somersaults!'

Maria isn't quite at the point of turning somersaults, but she is very excited by this sentimental journey and wants to show me every square inch of her childhood. We clamber about the courtyards and the fields, Maria leaning on my arm for balance, but amazingly agile despite her lame foot. On these uneven surfaces, in fact, her lameness is barely noticeable, nothing like what it must have been in her childhood, when one foot, straightened out by surgery only twelve years ago, was still folded over on itself, the ankle bent at a right angle by polio.

I was only about two when I had polio, I don't remember it at all. I only recall one thing about having polio – that my father used to take me to the orthopaedic hospital here in Trapani for a sort of electric shock treatment, and we'd go by cart. But if this happened in '42 or in '43, I couldn't say. I only remember that once we were going to Trapani in the cart, me, my father, and maybe one of my uncles. And anyway, there was a bombing, and a fragment of one of these bombs hit the mule and tore his ear off. The mule began to run away, and I can remember that my father grabbed hold of me and held me tight. But it's sort of like a vision, you know. Sometimes I make a real effort to remember things precisely, but I can't recall anything else about having polio.

And then, well, when I went to school, yes. The school was in Buzzarocca, down the road a piece from the baglio. We went on foot. And I remember the first time we went to school, the first day I went to school, my classmates started calling me names, they started shouting, 'Cripple! Cripple! Cripple!' And for a moment I felt bad. Then I said to myself, 'Why are they calling me that? I can walk all the same, I can do the same things they can, so why are they calling me that?' And as soon as they started calling me cripple again, I said to them, 'It's not true that I'm crippled, because I walk', I said, 'like you do, I do the same things you do, I play the games you play, so there! I'm *not* a cripple!' And after that they didn't make it hard for me. You know how it is, the first impact when there are children, but not afterwards. I didn't even have any trouble because I couldn't wear a shoe – I had to wear slippers all the time, because I couldn't get my foot into a shoe. But they never gave me any more trouble. I don't know why . . .

I had to get dressed up to go to school, and then undressed again when I came home. I mean as soon as I got home, my mother made me take off my dress, because I didn't have anything else to wear to school the next day, I only had the one dress. And my mother would wash that dress and put it carefully out to dry, so the next morning I was all nice and clean, with my smock. Blue it was, a blue smock with a white bow. And then we didn't have schoolbags, because my mother couldn't afford to buy them, so my grandmother made me a schoolbag out of burlap or something like that. And she made the handle out of a sort of vine, you know those vines that grow up olive trees sometimes? She made this handle and she covered it with material, and it seemed just like a proper handle. She made me a schoolbag to take to school, and I was so pleased.

I liked school. A lot. I was sorry that I couldn't continue. A while back I found one of my report cards: all eights and ten for good conduct. I wasn't naughty, but I've always been lively, and a tomboy. Playing with dolls, playing with pieces of material, sitting quietly next to my grandmother – because my grandmother wanted to teach me how to sew – that wasn't for me. Yes, I would go and sit, but as soon as she turned her back, I ran off. Or, for instance, she would comb my hair, she'd neaten me all up and put a bow in my hair, because in those days everyone wore bows. So I'd let her do it to make my grandmother happy, but as soon as I went out of the house, the bow was on the ground and underfoot. I was always like that. I didn't like the games that little girls played. I was always looking for something new; if I saw a couple of ants come out of a hole, for instance, I could sit on the ground for hours and watch those ants, see where they were going, what they were carrying home to eat, and so on. Just to give you an example. But I couldn't sit still and sew.

Or, for instance, if I found a flower growing, the next day I'd go back to see how big it had gotten. There were these flowers then – we all called them *chicchi ri 'addu*, tiny, tiny flowers, the red ones that come up in the spring? I don't know what they're called in Italian.* I used to spend hours with those flowers. I used to watch them grow, I'd go back the next day, I'd count them, and then I'd pick them and pull them all apart to see how they were made. Kids' games, really!

There was a gravel pit near there, they used to quarry gravel there to dump on the roadbeds. We made a slide there, my brother Nardo and I, and we'd climb up to the top and go sliding, we'd sit down on the edge and zzrrrooom! And our bottoms torn to pieces! You should get Nardo to tell you. Every day, every single day we went and tore a pair of under-pants on our grandmother. Every blessed day. It was a thing with us. Zzzsssttt! And down we'd go. Then we'd run around back up again, and vrrrooom! Or we'd find a piece of rope and play jump rope with it. These were our games.

My grandmother used to have talcum powder that came in a flat tin box, and she took the bottom out of one of these tins and made it into a hoop, an embroidery hoop, and she put some material over it, to teach me how to embroider. I took it and threw it: vrrrooom! Because I wasn't made for

* Scarlet pimpernel, *Anagallis arvensis L.*

that kind of work. If someone said to me, 'Go work in the fields!' I'd go. If they said to me, 'Cook dinner!' I'd cook. I cooked a lot when I was a little girl. 'Make some pasta!' I'd make pasta. How much pasta we cranked out, my brother Nardo and I, when we were little! With the *arbitrio*? The machine you make pasta with? You knead it by hand, and then you put it in the top of this machine and turn a handle and the pasta comes out underneath. How much pasta we made! We used to make *ditali* and *anelletti* and spaghetti – and noodles, I learned to cut noodles, too.

We ate pasta every day, every evening. We'd make *taglierini*, or very thin little *tagliarelli*. We'd have pasta with fava beans in the evenings, and then on Sundays we'd have pasta with tomato sauce. On weekdays always pasta with dried beans, or greens, or cauliflower when there were cauliflowers, or with potatoes, which we grew ourselves.

In those days you made your own pasta and bread at home. I remember after the threshing they'd bring the wheat home in big sacks, and when it was time to go to the mill they'd take a couple of measures of grain, two or three decalitres, sort it, and put it in to soak, then spread it out on rugs in the sun to dry. Once it was dry, my father took it to be ground into flour.

Well, bygone times. Good times, bad times, who knows? For us kids, maybe because we were stupid, they were good times. There was hunger, there was poverty, but I remember them as good times. We were in the country, we had fun, it was . . . sincere. We played with the most ordinary things. I remember how shoe polish used to come in little tins and when they were empty we'd take these and make a hole with a nail and make saucepans, to play with. There were the *panopoli* bushes* that have those little tiny red berries, and if we played at making ragout, these were the meatballs, or whatever. That's what we played with. We could play with them all day long. Or we'd make carts and wagons out of the paddles from the prickly pears. These were our games. And then there was always the mare. My father had a horse, he had a mare, he had a mule. How we loved to go riding!

I don't remember the mare's name, only her colour, she was a sorrel. The mule's name was Zazà, but maybe the mare didn't have a name. We rode her, not the mule, because he kicked. Me up front and my brother Nardo behind, we'd ride round and round the houses, or we'd ride down into the valley where there was a little shop and we'd go buy soap or a spool of thread, we'd go on horseback. We'd go visit my uncle, or my grandmother.

We had these games, and then we had to work. We always worked: hoisting water from the well, how much water I must have hoisted, there was no end to it. Once my brother Nardo and I, we did something naughty. There was a great big well in the middle of the baglio, I don't know if it's still there. We set out to play – because you have to play at that age, too – and we made a swing in the well. We found a wooden beam and we put it with one end on one side of the well and the other end on the other side of the well and we climbed out on the beam and let ourselves down by our hands. And we swung back and forth inside the well!

My grandmother, as soon as she saw what we were doing,

* *Myoporum serratum.*

she didn't say anything – she just called, '*Bring me some water immediately, I need some water!*' And when we brought the water she started in: 'What a thing! My grandchildren down the well!' We never did it again. For we used to pay attention to what our grandmother told us.

And we used to go and gather the wood to cook with, my brother Nardo and I, with a big basket we'd go and gather wood. And we'd go and get water for washing, for cooking, for everything. We had to hoist it, Nardo and I, with a bucket, like this, hand over hand. We had a copper tub: a handle for me and a handle for my brother, and we'd bring the water to my grandmother. How often I used to stand next to my grandmother, when I was still little, and scrub the laundry in the wash tub! I wasn't tall enough to reach, so she'd put a stool for me to climb on, and I'd scrub.

Yet those were good times. We had pasta to eat every day, and on Sundays with tomato sauce, and sometimes an egg in it. But rarely. My mother, my grandmother, they had baskets where they kept the eggs that the hens laid, since when they needed a length of material, when they bought soap, or a spool of thread, or a kerchief, they paid for it with eggs.

Yes, there were olive trees on our land. We used to cure the olives with salt. We had olive trees, we had a little olive oil, but we used it by the drop. When we had pasta and fava beans, for example, we didn't put any oil on it, to save. Those were hard times then. At noon we ate bread, a slice of bread with another little piece of bread on top, and that was our cheese. That's what we ate: olives that we'd cured ourselves, salted olives, or salad, cardoons – I remember going to pick cardoons with my grandmother, and then we'd eat them with a little *agghia*, a pesto of garlic and tomatoes. Then, for instance, we'd eat sardines that we'd salted ourselves, a little piece of mackerel that we'd salted at home, or else in the tuna season, we'd get tunafish. My father would go to the tunnery at Bonagia to buy it, he'd do some odd jobs to earn enough to buy the *tracchi*, that's what we called them, the gills of the tunafish. And we used to salt these gills, and if anyone wanted some salt fish he'd have that. I don't remember anything else. Bread and tomatoes.

The cheese we had to sell. We didn't have any money. In those days a notebook for school cost five lire. My father would give us the money, but when we went to school we'd spend it on a square of chocolate. One square cost two and a half lire, and with the other two and a half lire we'd buy some little cookies, cookies that came in the form of the alphabet. Little cookies, A, B, C, D, or else numbers. For example, with two lire you could get ten or twenty cookies, and then we'd fight, my brother Nardo and I, over how to divide them up. But he always got more, and me less. These are my memories of childhood.

The whole family was together; almost everyone lived nearby. On Christmas Day, or Easter, or New Year's, I remember my mother would dress us up – this was out in the country and there was a lot of mud, but she'd dress us up all neat and clean, and send us off hand in hand, and we'd go and kiss the hands of our grandparents. As soon as it was light, we went to kiss their hands. For the important feast days, Christmas, Easter, New Year's, you had to kiss the hands of your aunts and uncles, of your father and mother, and of your grandparents.

My mother used to say to us, 'When you go to your grandfather's, you mustn't ask for anything. Don't ask for a thing.' You had to behave yourself. And on the feast days we all went to eat dinner at my grandfather's – for Carnival, for example. The morning of Carnival we had fried pork, the innards of the pig and pieces of the meat, everyone around a big table, my grandfather at the head of the table and the meat in a great bowl in the middle. Then around four o'clock we'd have ragout with pork meat, with all the rind and all the bones, pork with tomato sauce. Made with tomato extract, though. Do you know what tomato extract is? It's sauce that is turned into concentrate by being dried in the sun. It has a wonderful taste. And instead of putting sugar in it – we didn't have any sugar, there wasn't any money and we couldn't buy sugar – my grandmother made a concentrate of prickly pear fruit, and when she made the extract she added some. That way it was a little sweeter. Actually this concentrate of prickly pear was used only for that, for the tomato extract, but Nardo and I, we used to take some when nobody was looking and spread it on our bread.

And so we'd all go and eat at my grandfather's. All our uncles were there: one had four children, one had five children, one had six children, so we were a great big family. And once my brother Nardo got left without any meat, because he was the smallest of the bunch, maybe – anyway he didn't get any meat, and so as soon as everyone had finished eating he went and burst into tears. And my mother: 'Why are you crying?' and Nardo: 'Grandfather didn't give me any meat.' In the end he got more meat than anybody!

Each family killed its pig for Carnival. In the morning we'd eat this fried pork with lemon squeezed on it, and then about four in the evening ragout, pasta with tomato sauce and pork meat. And then, for instance, every family made its own sausage, we'd make lard, you know? Salt lard with pepper in it – wonderful with a piece of bread. We'd salt the rind, too, and cook up a piece with our beans in wintertime – nothing of that pig got thrown away! And then we ate all these things.

This was my childhood.

4

The bitter wind that blew across the hill at Ballata was a good antidote to the glow of nostalgia, reminding me that Maria must have spent a good part of her early childhood feeling cold and hungry and wistful. But she was loved, and she was free to run as best she could and to ride, to play as well as to work. The Sicilian sun can be warm even in winter, and when a holiday came she had a plate of meat and all her family around her. The more she told me – the more clearly I could imagine her hobbling swiftly across the fields to school with Nardo running at her side, or picture the two of them riding on the little sorrel mare with Nardo clinging to his sister's waist, or hear their shrieks and laughter as they hurtled themselves down the side of the gravel pit – the better I could grasp the trauma of her entering the San Carlo.

I wasn't yet eleven when my father died. He died of a heart attack. He was fine when he left for the fields in the morning, and he was brought home dead. My brother came to the house saying, 'Mamma, you have to go to the doctor's!' He didn't tell me anything, and he was younger than me.

What were we to do? There were six of us at home. My mother had a pension, 6,200 lire every two months, and with that she had to maintain a family of six children. My brother Nardo, the oldest of the boys, went to work in the fields with an uncle; I and my six-year-old sister entered the San Carlo.

It was in August, the first of August 1952, that my father died, and there were five of us, plus my mother was two months pregnant with my sister Pina. There were people who wanted me as a servant, to work for them, but my mother kept saying, 'No, no, and no! My daughters may go hungry but they'll go hungry in my house, for I'm not going to send them out in service.' Then my uncle heard that there was this institute here in Erice, and so they brought us to Erice. To the San Carlo. We were supposed to be admitted after Christmas. But my uncle said, 'Wouldn't it be better to take them there before Christmas? That way they'd be there for Christmas and they'd have more to eat.' And so on the twentieth of December they took us there, the twentieth day of December. And that was that.

It was terrible leaving our mother. She didn't come with us, it was my uncle, my father's brother, who took us there. All dressed in black with our black veils, we went to the San Carlo. And when we went in and I saw all those iron grates and things, I wanted to run away. I was only a child . . .

So, we entered, my uncle left us between the gate and the inner door, because he wasn't allowed to come inside, and there we were. It was Suor Stellina who took charge of us, she became a sort of second mother to me. She took us in charge because we slept in the same dormitory where she slept, she made us take a bath in a big tub, we put on our uniforms, and there we stayed. I couldn't sleep at night; we were both of us in one bed, my sister and I, me at the head and she at the foot. In the evening we'd get into bed and put our arms around each other and cry, because we wanted our mother, we missed our father, and it was at least a week before we began to settle. I would say to my sister, 'Don't be frightened, my love, look, what's Mamma to do? What's she to do with all the other children to take care of? We two have to stay here, we've got to. What else can we do?' It was horrible, horrible because then Christmas came, there was a Christmas atmosphere even there, made out of nothing, but still you could feel it. I was really attached to my family, 'specially to my little brother Fanino, I'd brought him up, and I kept thinking about him. I wanted to throw myself out of a window.

And then we didn't have any news from home. After a month had passed my uncle came to visit, and we said to him, 'Why doesn't our mother come? Why doesn't Mamma come?' They never told us why our mother wouldn't come to see us, so after about two months, I started saying to my sister, 'You see? Mamma's not coming. Mamma doesn't think about us any more.' I started to resign myself, I'd tell myself, 'My mother brought us here and she never thinks about us.' But later, after the baby was born, our mother came to visit us. And when she did, I took it badly, I didn't even want to say hello to her, because she had abandoned us there and had never come to see us. My sister no, my sister threw herself into my mother's arms. Maybe it was because I was bigger, I understood more. I said to her, 'You had your other children, you forgot about us, you brought us here and you left us.' She said to me, 'I couldn't come to see you.' 'Why

82

not, why couldn't you?' I asked. 'Because I was having your sister, I was pregnant, with a big belly, and they didn't want me to come and see you like that.' And so I realized that my mother hadn't come to see us because the nuns had forbidden her to come. Because otherwise we would have seen her with a big belly. And it seemed so absurd to me, so old-fashioned. What about when my brother Fanino was born? I remember when he was born. I didn't actually see him being born, but I remember it all: my grandmother was there, they were getting the water and the linen ready. We were in the next room and as soon as the baby was born, my grandmother carried him in for us to see. She held him in her arms and showed him to me, I remember it all. So why? Why shouldn't we girls have seen our mother's belly?

But the nuns were like that. They used to fight with each other and carry on because they were envious, they were jealous. Holy Mother! A bunch of gossips! Maybe life in the convent seemed so serene to us because we took everything in a different manner, not like them. After all, most of these nuns had been put into the convent because their fathers had died or something like that, like Ministra. She was so beautiful, and she was only sixteen when her father died and they brought her there. Then, when she was twenty-one, she decided to stay there. But I don't think it was because she had a vocation. I don't know what it was.

There was Suor Francesca, she was just like a child. She didn't have any meanness in her, she stayed like she was. She entered the San Carlo when she was seven years old, and she never left. The first time she left the convent was when they made a new law that the nuns had to go out to vote, and when she went out into the middle of the street it made her dizzy. She'd never been out! And she was already in her eighties when I knew her.

Suor Luigia was like that too, she had entered the convent when she was very young and she never left. For her it was inconceivable that little boys were shaped differently from little girls. It was inconceivable. She had never seen a little boy naked. When my sister went out to school, and Suor Luigia helped her with her homework, she was shocked by the pictures in my sister's reader. What could there have been in an elementary school reader in those days? I ask you!

Suor Stellina wasn't really a nun. She went in when her mother died, but she never really became a nun. She was a little more sensitive towards us, but the nuns weren't. It wasn't that in their hearts they were evil. It was because that was their world, maybe – I can't really explain it, not even to myself.

They had no sympathy with the problems of children, for that's what we were, after all, children. It was a shock for me, I don't know if I've ever told you, but I had a terrible shock. I was so hurt, and even now, now that I'm more than fifty years old, I think about it and wonder how I could have been so innocent. I got my period when I was fourteen. I knew *nothing!* So I went to one of the nuns and told her and she said – it wasn't as if she told me that it was a menstrual cycle and so on – she said to me, 'Pray to the Madonna that it will go away.' So I went into the church to pray to the Madonna – what a nightmare! And when my period stopped I said to myself, 'The Madonna has heard my prayers! The Madonna has heard my prayers!' The next month was a terrible shock to me. I never confided in that nun again. And it wasn't until

I was eighteen or so that I realized that this was a regular monthly cycle, that it was normal. My mother had never told me about these things, first of all because I was little, and then because you didn't talk about these things in those days. But if my mother had been there she would have explained everything to me. Not like the nun. These are things, little episodes that I still think about . . .

In those days we'd been through a war, and there were a lot of poor people at Erice, who used to come with little saucepans, to ask for a ladle of pasta. The kitchen was full of these little pans. We'd put a little pasta in each, and the ones who had little children, the ones who had problems, would come and get them, that way they'd have a plate of hot pasta. But there were those in the convent who only ladled out the broth, no pasta. I thought that was a terrible thing to do. When I was on kitchen duty, I used to wait till the nun had her back turned and if there was any raw pasta left over I'd add it to the pot. The nun would come and say, 'Well? The pasta that was here?' 'It was so little, I put it in the pot,' I would say. 'What did you go and do that for!' What a lot of scoldings! How many times I had to do penance, on my knees in the middle of the refectory at mealtime!

There was a little boy who used to come to the door of the oven room. He's like a brother to me to this day, his name is Settimo. When he came with his father to deliver the firewood, he was only about seven or eight. There were some wooden steps in the oven room, and he'd sit down there and wait. 'What's wrong, Settimo?' I'd ask him. 'I'm hungry,' he'd say to me, 'a little bread and cheese?' So I'd take some bread and some cheese and give it to him. Then the nun would come: 'Where's the cheese gone?' 'I gave it to Settimo because he was hungry.' 'Why did you give it all to him? Couldn't you have given him less? A sliver, that's what you should have given him!'

This is a vocation? This is charity? This is apostolate? No, ma'am, as far as I'm concerned the apostolate is something outside the church, it's walking, meeting someone, giving them a smile, a kind word. That's what it is for me.

Suor Domitilla, when she died, she was almost a hundred years old. She died just like that, in her sleep, on Corpus Christi Day. When we all sat down to dinner in the refectory – it was a big room, next to the kitchen, with a table shaped like a horseshoe – for dinner on Thursdays and Sundays, there was pasta asciutta with tomato sauce, and Suor Domitilla wanted the sugar bowl on the table in front of her, because she liked to put sugar on her pasta instead of cheese. When I was on kitchen duty, I'd forget and put out the cheese bowl. Then there were fireworks! She would stand in the middle of the refectory and shout, '*Ladruna di muntagna!* Mountain bandit!' That was me, because I came from the country. 'So you want to sell the sugar and leave me with the cheese!' And when we had finished eating she would stand up and say – and she was quite a figure, very tall and heavy – '*Mangiasti, bevisti, ma da me 'un ci venisti!* You ate, you drank, but you didn't come to me!' Which meant that it was time to go into church and thank the Lord for what he had given us to eat. That Corpus Christi Day, after we'd said our prayers in church she went to take a nap, and we found her like that, dead in her sleep.

Then there was Suor Maria Angela, she was the last one. At the end Suor Maria Angela was the last nun left alive. Then there was one who used to pee all over herself, Suor

Luigia. She peed in her pants, she couldn't feel it any more. When we went into church, and she put a *cuffuna* with coals in it under her skirts, the smell of the hot cloth all soaked in pee was enough to kill you! We used to take lighted cuffune into the church when we went to say our rosaries, to keep our feet warm. And the hem of her skirts would end up in the coals, and the smell of the burning cloth was something terrible. Sometimes we girls would take the wooden spools that Suor Angela used for making lace, and throw them into the nuns' cuffune so they'd catch fire. 'Gesù! Gesù! My skirts are on fire!' We used to laugh when they pulled their skirts up, because they wore those old-fashioned drawers split on the sides, with ties at the waist that came round, the back piece tied at the front, and the front tied at the back.

We would put the spools in the coals. 'Madonna mia! I'm burning up!' They'd pull up their skirts to see where the fire was, and we would laugh to see those funny drawers. When I was bigger, and I slept in the same room as the Ministra, she got so fat that she couldn't reach to tie her drawers in the back, and she'd put her habit on over them without the belt and then call me behind the screen. 'Come tie these things for me, will you?' So I used to see her drawers with the splits in them. And then we'd see them hanging out to dry. The past! When I think about it now it seems like a dream. Are these really things that happened to me?

They were really simple, those nuns, they didn't know anything about the world, about what was happening outside. In 1960 the president of the ECA bought us a radio, but as soon as the nuns turned it on, and heard these people talking: 'No! Turn off that radio! Those people will hear us! We don't want those people in our house!' It seems incredible, but it's true. We couldn't ever turn on the radio because we weren't supposed to let those people in.

But the outside world didn't attract me. No. Because in my heart I thought that the world ended there, within those four walls and that was that. For me the world was those four walls. Or maybe they drilled it into us so when we were little, gave us such a brainwashing, I don't know. But that was the world. They taught us that everything was sinful, that everything was illicit, whatever we did. Even for instance if you had the desire to eat a piece of fruit, that was greed and it was a sin. You were supposed to mortify your appetites, and punish them. If you used the bidet, you had to wash yourself with a sponge, because it was sinful to touch yourself. Just to give you a stupid example. You weren't supposed to look in the mirror. Vanity! The devil would look out at you. In the summer, for instance, even though you were hot, you had to wear a short-sleeved undershirt, in case somebody might see the hair in your armpits – in your own bedroom! That would be a sin! It's true, brainwashing is what it was. You weren't supposed to wear a bra, ever. At the San Carlo one didn't use a bra, what was this business of lifting up your breasts? You should wear a corset to flatten you out, not something to lift you up. It would be vanity to show off your breasts.

There was a girl at the San Carlo named Maria Franchini, who started developing, and one of the nuns thought that her uniform showed off her breasts too much. 'So! Do you think you're going to the procession like that? I'll show you!' She laced Maria's corset really tight, so tight that it was very painful, and Maria started crying. 'Why are you crying?' I asked. 'She laced me flat and it hurts!' 'And you keep it that way? Who do you think is going to be looking at you?' She wasn't supposed to go in the procession in a dress that made her breasts look big. She was only fourteen years old and her breasts were growing, all squashed in so that they hurt. That's a proper thing to do? Phooey!

Once this Maria Franchini and I, we got hold of an old burner and a canister of gas, the one they used to use to heat up the milk for the priest, to make him a cappuccino when he had finished hearing our confessions. We hid this burner in the closet behind the bathroom, and one day when we had pasta with cauliflower, some cauliflower was left over. So Maria said, 'Let's make cauliflower fritters.' So we stole a little flour, just enough to make a batter for these fritters, and we took a pan and a little oil from the kitchen. Other times we'd make a salad, we'd steal a tomato, for example, and a sardine and we'd make ourselves a salad. We had to eat, didn't we? Growing girls made to fast like that! So that's what we did. Then one day Titì came and spied on us while we were at it. The nun came and she took everything that we had and she threw it down the toilet.

Maria Franchini was really something. When Suor Maria Angela walked around the refectory, Maria would walk behind, mimicking her. The very image! Maria copied her exactly, all her ways – because Suor Maria Angela was always so cross, we used to call her the Bear. She had bangs on her forehead that stuck out from under her veil, and when they turned white she started dying the ends of her bangs with shoe polish, so that it looked like her hair was still black. But when she was on oven duty and she sweated, all the black ran down onto her face.

We got into the habit, Maria and I: we'd steal a tomato, we'd steal half a sardine, or a little bit of cheese, and then we would go up onto the terrace when we got out of church, after prayers. In the summer we'd go up onto the terrace. 'Where have those pumpkinheads got to now?' – which meant they were looking for us, and we'd hide ourselves and start eating. A slice of cheese. Can you imagine? That's what we stole, a slice of cheese. Bread we never stole, they gave us half a kilo a day, more than we wanted. We wanted something different. The food was always the same: beans, cauliflower, beans, cauliflower, and then sometimes they'd give us peas. You know the kind? The dried split peas? They always stuck to the pot and burned. The stink was enough to kill you. Down the toilet! Phooey! We managed to survive, though, that's for sure.

5

In the course of my many visits to Maria's kitchen, I have seen some of the ghosts from her past materialize. A tiny old woman with a dark blue smock under her coat and white hair pulled back into a wisp of braided knot turns out to be Ninetta. She drops in one afternoon while pasta di conserva is in the works, and it seems almost an automatic reflex for her to take off her coat, sit down, and start making marzipan rosebuds alongside the others. She has very naughty black eyes, and although she pretends to be embarrassed by the story of the sanitary napkins – 'Can't you tell her something else!' – it still makes her giggle.

Fifth in a family of six sisters, Ninetta was the darling of an aunt who was a nun at the San Carlo and who had taken care of her during a childhood illness. When Ninetta finished elementary school, the aunt suggested that she come to live with her in the institute. By the time Maria entered the San Carlo, Ninetta was almost thirty years old, and the even pace of work and religious observance, enlivened by occasional minor assertions of her seniority, was apparently very satisfying to her. Unlike Maria, Ninetta is still an assiduous churchgoer: her only resentment appears to be directed towards 'them' – the authorities who closed the institute and threw her out onto the street when she was almost fifty with nothing (Ninetta lives with a sister in a house that belongs to them) but her crooked hands (she waves her fingers, gnarled by work and by age, at me). And, one is tempted to add, her uniform: I have never seen Ninetta without a dark blue smock.

It seems extraordinary that someone with parents and property should choose orphanhood as a career, a reminder that the prospects for the women of a Sicilian village in the 1930s were not that much better or more varied than they had been in the Middle Ages or the Renaissance, when wealthy nuns were allowed to move from dormitories into single cells built with their own funds – which were then inherited by nieces co-opted into the convent for that purpose. And that to someone of an acquiescent character, the San Carlo offered community, serenity, security.

Maria was anything but acquiescent. She had intelligence, curiosity, and an independent, even rebellious spirit, combined with a strong sense of family responsibility. But an extremely circumscribed youth had denied her the information necessary to rational choice. Everything had to be battled out on another level.

The first time that I got leave to go out from the San Carlo was after I'd been in there four years. Leave to go home for the day, that is, to my house at Erice. For after my father died, first my mother went to stay at Chiesanuova, to be near her mother. Then after my sister Pina was born, her uncles advised her to move: 'Why don't you go up to Erice? What are all these children going to do here? Up there they'll have a better chance to find work.' So Mamma rented a house in Erice. 'I want to be near my daughters,' she said. And she would come almost every other day to see us, behind the grate, it's true, but she got to see us. And when we were bigger she was allowed to come inside sometimes, or else sometimes she'd cook something for us at home and bring it to us.

So she came up to Erice, and my brother Berto went to work after school for the tobacconist, who had a bar; Berto delivered coffee and things, and was paid 500 lire a day. Three hundred he'd give to my mother to buy bread, to buy pasta. And he went to school as well. Berto came after my sister Angela, he must have been about seven or eight when they moved to Erice. Then there was my brother Fanino and my sister Pina: my mother put them into the nursery school at San Pietro, where they gave them something to eat and kept them until four o'clock. And my mother went out to work as a washerwoman. She went out to do laundry, tubs of laundry! And they'd pay her 500 lire, 600 lire, something like that. Or they'd give her a half-kilo of pasta, a kilo of bread. And at four o'clock she'd come back because she had to go get the children at the nursery.

My mother had to come and ask the nuns for permission for me to go out, otherwise I couldn't. Not just to go home for Christmas Day or something like that: it had to be something important, like my cousin's wedding.

When I finally did leave the San Carlo, it was in order to go to Catania, and then I never went back again. I thought I had the vocation to become a nun, and I went to Catania where there was a cloistered order, a convent of Carmelite nuns. I entered, but not as a novice, only to see what it was like, and I got sick. I got something that I'd already had before, all my nerves went soft and I could only move one arm. I was an invalid. I woke up one morning and I couldn't feel my legs or anything. Maybe because I was unhappy that I'd gone there . . .

They called the doctor when it didn't go away, and he said that it was a nervous collapse due to a decline of the organism: I was wasting away. I'm healthy enough now. This was in about 1962, I was twenty-two, twenty-three years old, and I didn't have enough substance in my body to produce antibodies. I caught everything: if there was a cold going around, I was sure to catch it, and I always had a sore throat.

I had the same kind of decline when I was about fifteen, I always had a temperature. Of course I had a decline, since I didn't eat anything. I didn't want the milk. Milk? It was water! And I threw it in the toilet. Pasta with beans – I couldn't stand the smell, it was always burnt, and made a terrible smell. Or those fava beans – always sticking and burning. The smell was enough to kill you! So I got sick, my glands were all inflamed. It was a decline of the organism. They made all sorts of tests and then, after four or five months, I got better.

Maybe it was the diet at the San Carlo. Oranges? For Christmas! Maybe sometimes an apple. Do you think they gave us fruit? Nooo. Sure, if they were making conserva, then we'd steal a citron and eat it, or a tangerine if they were making rosolio. But the nuns used to buy fruit for themselves. There was a man named Bono who came by with a cart, and they'd buy themselves oranges, or tangerines, or dates – but not for us. I remember once my sister Angela saw a nun eating a tangerine, and she went and stood in front of her. 'Will you give me a piece?' – and she wouldn't give it to her. Wasn't that mean? I told my mother about it and she, poor thing, she went and bought us an orange. The nun bought tangerines for herself and wouldn't give us any, while my mother had to scrub other people's washing to buy them for us.

There was a family living near my mother that had a lot of money, they were from Trapani but they spent a lot of time in Erice. They had an only daughter, and when oranges or tangerines and things arrived from their estates, she would call to my sister Pina and say, 'Come here, my friend.' She let down a basket on a cord with oranges in it or tangerines, sweet fennel, grapes when they were in season, all the things that came in from their farms. Or if they cooked something special: 'Here, my friend, this is for you and your brother to eat.' For this kind of thing Erice was different, Erice kept an eye on children. Not on us at the San Carlo, since they thought that we were well fed . . . but on the young ones, on my brother Berto, on Fanino and Pina.

So I went to Catania to see this convent and I fell sick there. I don't remember how long I was there, but it was awful. The place itself was beautiful, but the life they led – worse than the one here! It was a cloistered order, you weren't allowed to talk, the blanket on the bed had a skull on it, and in the middle of the night they would come and knock on the door, you had to get up and go into the church for prayers. In the middle of the night! It was a nightmare.

And the nuns were just the same, maybe worse. They were always fighting among themselves, you could tell. And they didn't have any charity. So they were just a group of women stuck in together, but not because they loved their neighbour. This is why I don't go to church. It's not that I don't . . . I mean I still believe. I don't go to church because Jesus said to us, 'Love thy neighbour like thyself.' But if you behave like that, how can you go to church and pray to the Lord? If you see someone in the middle of the street who's in need, and you turn your back on him, how can you be religious? You tell me I have to be religious and then you turn your back on people! At least that's the way I see it. Or you eat while your neighbour goes hungry. A slice for you and a slice for me. How can you eat a tangerine with a child standing and watching you, what kind of Christian charity is that? And as soon as you finish eating, you go into the church to pray. But for what, to whom are you praying? These are what I call sins. Or the way we were growing girls, we needed to eat, and they kept the good milk for themselves and gave us half milk and half water. Was that right? The way they would make pasta and cauliflower, and in our plates they'd put a ladle of broth and a couple of strands of pasta, and fill their own plates up full: 'They won't eat it anyway.' Why wouldn't we eat it? Because it was dishwater! The way they'd serve themselves first and then, when they saw there wasn't enough broth left for us, they'd add a little water, cold water! So what were we, dogs? I don't even treat my dogs like that.

That experience in Catania was horrible, but I had wanted to try it. Maybe those nuns were . . . or maybe it's that I never really and truly had the vocation to become a nun. What sad people, too sad. Sometimes deep down inside I hate them, these nuns, and then I don't hate them. I don't even know myself. I try not to blame them. Life isn't like that. That was one period of my life, and that's that. Then there was another period, then another period, and then still another period. That was just one period of my life, my childhood. It wasn't anyone's fault, it happened like that. I can't give the blame to anyone.

And then, in a certain sense, I can say that those were the best years of my life. The years at the San Carlo, how carefree they were! You had a bed and a piece of bread, you had them for sure – can you understand? That's what was important, to have a piece of bread. In those days.

And I'm thankful to them for what they taught me, for they did, they taught me something with which to earn a living. But actually I had to steal that as well, by watching here and watching there, because the nuns were very jealous. I used to spend days watching at the table in the workroom. It was a big, long table and everyone sat around it working and they didn't want us little ones, we had to stand back if we wanted to watch. I wanted to learn because I liked these things and so I used to kneel like this with my hands and my chin on the edge of the table. I'd go next to where Suor Stellina was working and I would kneel like that so that I didn't get in her light. On my knees! And Titì would say, 'Look! The little doggie has come to beg!' But what else could I do? How else could I learn?

When you're young it's different, when your memory's good. All I had to do was watch once while they made something, and I had the recipe written here in my head. I didn't bring away one single thing from there, not one written recipe, not even an old marzipan mould. All I have is what they taught me, what's in my head, and I stole that.

The riches that were there in the San Carlo, it was one of the richest institutions in Erice! I'd like to know where it all went. There isn't anything there any more. All the furnishings and paintings and silver from the churches of Erice that were being closed were all brought to the San Carlo to keep. Where have they all gone? There's nothing left there.

When I entered the San Carlo and the ECA gave me my wardrobe and my sheets, they gave me a wooden chest to keep them in. When I left, since there were no more girls entering, I asked for it: 'Would you give me this chest?' But they didn't want to give it to me. All those years it had stood at the foot of my bed, I wanted it as a keepsake, but they wouldn't give it to me. It hurt not to have anything of my own.

When I opened my own shop I went and told them what I was doing, and Suor Stellina wouldn't speak to me. They were jealous that I was opening a shop of my own. They were jealous. And once I went and asked for one of their old moulds, one I didn't have, and they wouldn't give it to me, they wanted to keep it all for themselves. I only wanted to borrow the mould, I didn't want to keep it for ever, just borrow it to copy. Maybe it was the mould for the lamb, I don't remember. Anyway I made one for myself. I made the lamb by hand and then I took some plaster and made a mould of it. I still have it today.

But it took enormous willpower. To get where I am today has taken an enormous effort. Because I wanted it with all my strength, with all my will.

One of the sources of this strength is manifest in Maria's kitchen: Nardo, the little brother who tagged along or rode behind, has become an immense boulder of a man; tall for a Sicilian and heavyset. His hair has gone completely white, making him seem older than his fifty years, and some of his muscles have ceded to fat in the four or five years since he has been working for Maria. His solidity and imperturbability provoke an immediate desire to lean on him.

Nardo worked for many years as the custodian of an explosives deposit, which furnished the dynamite for the marble quarries in the hills north of Erice. It was an excellent job, he told me, but he decided to leave because it was making him too nervous. I readily sympathized, but it turned out that I had misunderstood: it wasn't the dynamite that made him nervous, but the bookkeeping. Every time a Mafia bomb went off in Palermo, the police would descend upon the deposit, and Nardo became convinced that if he erred by as much as a decimal point, he would end up in jail. So he came to work for Maria.

Working next to Maria's volatile temperament is not totally unlike working next to explosives, and Nardo handles his sister with the same calm that stood him in good stead earlier, and with a devotion that is touching in its quiet intensity and its sensitivity. He shares his sister's love of reminiscing, and drifts in and out of our conversations, confirming or contradicting what Maria is telling me in an often telling counterpoint.

So my sister left the San Carlo and opened the shop down the street, across the alley from the San Salvatore. I was working with a construction company then, and in the evenings I'd go over to the shop. There wasn't much trade, she sold a few pastries, she made mostaccioli, and then the evenings we'd make pizza, pizzettas, that sort of thing, and sell them there. It wasn't much, real small. Then the situation improved, it grew, and we moved up here.

Maria was born in '40, I in '42. When our father died, I went to work in the fields with an uncle of ours. I stayed with him from '52 until '59 and I only earned my keep. He gave me my food and my clothing – and an education. He taught me to behave myself, you could say, because in those days, with the hunger that there was, it didn't take much for an innocent lad to go wrong, to choose a bad road. But none of us, thank God, have ever taken that road.

In '59 I came up here to Erice, because I could see that agriculture was going backwards. My mother was already here, she moved up here to be closer to the girls, to Maria and Angela. My brother Berto began to work for the tobacconist after school, Pina started school, and then I came up. So we were together again, then Maria came out of the San Carlo, then after a year Angela came out too, the San Carlo closed, and we have gotten to where we are now.

But for you, Maria, your real family was the San Carlo. When you went to Catania you went against the will of Ministra, of Suor Maria Angela, of everyone there. Mamma didn't want you to go, and as for me, I didn't even say goodbye to you. I didn't see the sense of your becoming a cloistered nun. I couldn't understand why, why you should become a nun in a cloistered order. When you went there, it was all negative for you. But before you went and had a breakdown, a breakdown that was so bad for you, you should have said, 'Stop! I can't take this. I'm leaving!' Am I right or not? Instead you, rather than give anyone the satisfaction of hearing you say you were leaving, you said, 'I'm dying right here! I'm not going to give those women this satisfaction.' So it wasn't that you didn't like it here, or that you went there because you liked it there better. Am I wrong?

So in the meantime, Mary, she as good as died. That lady there meanwhile died. She as good as died, and the doctors took her to the hospital, to the Garibaldi Hospital in Catania. One evening – awful weather, raining and snowing – we got a telegram. We got a telegram saying that she was gravely ill and there was urgent and immediate need for us to go to Catania. I was still a boy, a lad – maybe I was twenty then. 'So she's sick,' I said, 'Mamma, let's go to Catania!' But my mother had a bad foot, she had a fistula between one toe and another. I said to myself, 'If I need help, she's not going to be able to give me much.' So I went to my mother-in-law – I was already engaged then – I went to her and I said, 'Will you come?' And she said yes. So the three of us went off to Catania, we went with Paoliddu Di Grazia in his hired car. When we got to Palermo, the highway police wouldn't let us go any farther because it was snowing and the roads were closed. So we looked around until we found the train station and we took the train. And we went to the Garibaldi Hospital and I found that lady there, paralysed, dead. Just like she was dead. Dead and buried. She couldn't talk, or open her eyes, or see or recognize or touch, she wasn't there. A nurse came and sent me to the doctor, who said, 'Either the mother or the eldest brother has to sign something, because we've got to make some experiments. We've got to draw off liquid from her spine, we've got to give her some electric shocks to see how she responds to the stimulus that we give her.'

I wasn't too convinced by all these things, and I said to myself, 'She's dead.' In my ignorance I said, 'She's as good as dead. If they give her electric shocks, she's just going to die faster.' So I said, 'No, I'm not going to sign anything, and neither is my mother. I'm taking my sister home with me.' He said, 'You can't touch her.' 'What do you mean I can't touch her? I can't have my sister? I can't take her home?' 'No.' 'Why not?' 'Your sister isn't in any condition to travel. As soon as you move her from there, just because you move her, she could expire and die, and you'd be guilty of attempted murder or manslaughter. You'd go to jail, thirty years and no-one could get you off.'

But we weren't signing anything and I kept saying, 'I'm going to take her home.' And when they couldn't stand it any longer they said, 'Take her! But you've got to sign a release.' I must have signed at least fifty papers – at least! I picked my sister up in my arms and I left. But how were we going to get to the station? I stole a chair that was standing in front of a shop across from the hospital, I stole the chair and sat her in it and carried her all the way to the station, chair and all. We got to the station and we took the train. And we came home, we came as far as Trapani by train, and then we took a taxi up the mountain. When we got up the mountain, there was snow everywhere, and it was about two in the morning. We got to Via Sales where we lived, and I pounded on the door for a long time, calling to my brother Berto who was inside and my brother Fano who was inside, asleep inside. I was making a noise like the devil but they didn't hear a thing. How could I keep her out in the snow? The taxi driver wanted to go home, what was I to do? So I went to my mother-in-law's house and we put her to bed there, at my mother-in-law's. She was still dead, though. She doesn't remember any of this.

She stayed at my mother-in-law's for a couple of weeks, until the weather got better, then I took her home. And I took her to be examined by Dr Tripi, who is a nerve doctor. He's still there, this doctor – at the insane asylum at Trapani. He charged 12,500 lire, at the time, 12,500 lire! So, he examined her, and he said to me, 'There is nothing wrong with her. There is nothing wrong with her at all.' And do you know what it was that cured her? The affection of her family, first of all, and a slice of horsemeat a day.

There was only one thing wrong with her. She had a nervous breakdown, a nervous decline – exhaustion. All her muscles had weakened and, in fact, after she'd been home for about three weeks, she started to get better. She had a head of hair that came down to here – have you ever seen the photograph? Her hair reached down to her bottom, and every morning before I went to work at six, I would comb her hair for her. Every morning. After she had been lying there at home dead, after a while, she began to move her fingers. I was really happy because she began to open her eyes and move her fingers a little bit. She doesn't remember those days. It was a bad experience. But it's not as if she went to become a nun saying to herself, 'If I like it there I'll stay.' She did it to spite something, or someone.

103

'I couldn't have done it to spite someone, I didn't have any motive for spiting anyone, nor could I have done it to spite my mother because she'd taken me there – my mother put me in the San Carlo for my own good.'

'So, why did you go away? Why? A disappointment in love, a . . .'

'A disappointment in love! I couldn't have had one then because I didn't know anyone. I never met anyone while I was in there. When I left the San Carlo, if they'd told me then, "Go throw yourself down the well," I'd have thrown myself down the well, because I didn't know anyone. I didn't know anything!'

'Am I right in saying that? I say that in order to get away, you had to let yourself go like that. What did you do to go into such a decline? You didn't eat, you didn't sleep, and why? Why do these things happen? Out of weakness and tiredness and stress. I mean someone who eats, who sleeps, who is happy, doesn't get these things.'

'In a life like that you couldn't be happy.'

'What life? Which life? The life in Catania?'

'Go on, the life in Catania! Life is a whole complex of things. You in your subconscious, you know that. After all, didn't you suffer the same thing that I suffered, this great upset, this being sent away from home?'

'But to go shut yourself up again, to shut yourself up, to open the door just in order to close it again, that was worse. I've never been able to understand that.'

'Yes, but I think that in my subconscious I thought that that was all there was to the world. To stay here or to stay there was the same thing.'

'You mean there was something wrong. It's useless for you to say no, Maria. There was something. Maybe you're not able to see what it was, but there was something wrong.'

'But not love! Not at that age!'

6

What remains to be told is the story of the shop. Maria's personal life after she left the convent – widowhood after only eight years of marriage, the great disappointment of remaining childless, a soured partnership with Angela, Berto, and Fanino – belongs to a world that is familiar. It has not been particularly happy. Great generosity – so easy to take for granted – combined with great drive – so hard to emulate – is not a recipe for family harmony, and small-town Sicilian society tends to be suspicious of success and social mobility.

But the shop is a happy place. When the afternoon sun pours in the back window, it shines on the glass doors of the old-fashioned cupboards, illuminates the platters heaped with almond pastries, lights on a few tourists, perhaps, sitting gratefully at one of the little marble-topped tables and resting their feet as they try a fig biscuit or a slice of crostata. The weathered grain chest holds a big vase of flowers surrounded by bottles of cordials, jars of preserves, baskets of multi-coloured Martorana, and across the room an ancient wooden *madia*, used for kneading bread and pasta dough, is filled with packages of biscuits.

At the front of the store, where the sun reaches only as it is setting, a long counter of gleaming wood and glass displays the whole wealth of Maria's heritage: the towering mounds of sospiri and bocconcini, the glistening chocolate of the dolcetti al liquore, the crystallized sparkle of the *palline all'arancio* and *al cioccolato*, the matte whiteness of powdered sugar on the crostate and the genovesi. And then the marzipan: the red, orange, and yellow of apples, oranges and bananas, green figs, the powdery bloom of peaches and apricots.

In the wintertime, when the tourists are rare and the bulk of trade is with the bars and cafés throughout the province of Trapani, the warmth generated by Maria's oven is an invitation to draw up a chair and chat. The kitchen is rarely without someone seeking a genovese and a bit of gossip: the owner of the antique shop across the street, the chef from the restaurant around the corner, Ninetta on her way home from Mass.

In spring and summer there is no space in the kitchen for idle chatter, and almost no room to elbow one's way through the bus loads of Germans, French, and even Japanese that crowd around the counter or line up at the back (as well as pastries, Maria's shop provides one of the few bathrooms available to people passing through Erice). For the tour companies, the shop is a blessing – an attractive (and toilet-equipped) place right on the main thoroughfare where their charges can purchase local specialities at reasonable prices – but the harried guides rarely take the time to tell the story behind it.

So my brother came and brought me to Erice. After a couple of months I got well again, but I didn't want to go back to the San Carlo, I realized that sooner or later it was going to close. And my mother agreed: 'Stay home, then. You can live here just the way we do.'

Meanwhile, the Bosco sisters – they were the ladies my mother rented her house from – the Bosco sisters asked me to make some Martorana for them. We had some almonds from our land at Carnevale, so I started making Martorana at home that first year, a little Martorana, a few pastries. Then I rented a room, not here where the shop is now, but a little farther down the street. I paid a carpenter 60,000 lire to make me a counter, and a mason built the oven for me. The firebricks cost 1,000 lire apiece. You need special firebricks for an oven, the kind that won't crack with the heat. The best ovens have a dome made out of pieces of old roof tiles, and the walls and floor built of firebricks. Under the bricks you put a layer of sand mixed with the ashes from a blacksmith's forge: that's the kind of oven that keeps the heat the longest.

And so I started, little by little. I opened the shop in 1964, on the first of June, but I didn't have any money to buy almonds. All I had was three kilos of almonds, three kilos of almonds to open a store with! So I made some pastries and I opened. And the end of the month came and the feast of Saint Peter and Saint Paul. I'd made mostaccioli, I'd made some biscuits, and just a few almond balls; I didn't have very many pastries, though. That day I took in 50,000 lire, and it seemed like an incredible sum to me. I'm talking about thirty years ago. Fifty thousand lire!

I bought 200 kilos of almonds – in those days they went at

about 600 lire a kilo, if I remember rightly – and I bought flour: I spent all I had on things for the store. If I had a rip in my stockings, I didn't care. And I went to work. My mother came to give me a hand. Since it was a wood-burning oven, my mother and my brother Berto helped me, we'd go down into the woods early in the morning to cut firewood. From that moment on, I told myself that I had to succeed. I had to because I *had* to! But it's not as if I could put anything into it, money or anything: just willpower.

And that's how I started in business: with a wood-burning oven, a hand-cranked nut grinder, and a rolling pin. Holy Mother! And so we started, little by little: this month I bought a knife, the next month another pastry sheet. We had to mix everything by hand, there was no machinery at all. Nothing, absolutely nothing! I'm a self-made woman: first I had the little shop, then in 1975 I opened a bigger shop, this one in via Vittorio Emanuele where I am now, and then I bought the other store, the one called the Pasticceria del Vecchio Convento, which my sister runs. That's a beautiful place, really beautiful, it was a church once, built in the four-teenth century. Then it was sold, they made a bakery there, then a grocery store, and then I turned it into a pastry shop. I did all this by myself, little by little.

Sure, it has taken sacrifice. I'm here until one in the morning sometimes. In the summer, in the tourist season when there's a lot of work, I'm here eighteen hours a day. But I do it with pleasure. It's a pleasure to me. And I'm still the same person I was twenty years ago. If I want to sit down in the middle of the shop and eat a sandwich, I go ahead and do it. I don't care. If I want to go out into the fields and pick wild mustard greens, I do it. I can't see anything wrong in it.

There are those who have to put on their fur coats to go to Mass on Sundays. I don't go to Mass. I'm religious but I don't go. I don't have a fur coat and I don't intend to buy one. This jacket is enough for me. It keeps the cold off and that's all I need. What we value has to be inside of us.

This sort of work, making the Christmas hearts, embroidering them with marzipan, it's an art that's disappearing. It's going to end. The other things will keep on going, but this is coming to an end. I, my sister, Titì, we know how to do it because we were all at the San Carlo. Young people today don't want to learn these things. For me, sitting here and making these things is really relaxing. They're so beautiful! And I like it because I'm creating something with my own hands, it's not like machine work, a robot that says, 'Do this! Do that!' Maybe that's why it relaxes me, because it's creating something. What do you think, will it disappear? No, it will, it will. The paschal lambs, all these things that are done by hand, you have to do them with such care, and you can't think about money while you're at it. You can't think about the money. Because if you keep thinking, 'I'm making this heart. For making this heart I'm going to earn 50,000 lire,' then you can't put in all the love that it takes, you're going to be thinking that the more hearts you make, the more you'll earn, and it won't come out right. You can't give it all the love it takes. Here at Erice nowadays all the young people want to study. You have to have an education, you have to have culture, but who learns a craft any more? Who learns an art? Everybody wants a desk job.

There's so much tradition in this. It's something that's been handed down; the merit isn't all mine. The merit belongs to others as well. I learned how, that's true, but it was the tradition that paved the way for me. Nobody cares any more. After I left the San Carlo, I presented a request to the town hall – I ran across a copy of the letter just the other evening – I asked for a corner of the San Carlo where I could keep the tradition alive and leave it to the town, but they refused. We're all scattered, me, my sister, Titì. Why couldn't they have gotten us all together and left the tradition there in the San Carlo where it was born?

The Recipes

The recipes that follow represent a complete inventory of the products Maria makes to sell in her shop, plus a couple for festive dishes that she remembers from her childhood. Or at least this is the entire inventory at the time of writing: Maria frequently experiments with new recipes or pastries that she has tasted elsewhere, and not all of the recipes given here date back to her years at the Istituto San Carlo. We have not given instructions for the fancy marzipan pieces that require a long apprenticeship, such as the paschal lambs, the Christmas hearts, or the pasta di conserva, although the ingredients are here for anyone with ambition and a knack for modelling.

The recipes fall into seven categories. There are six recipes for the basic doughs and fillings that, in various shapes and combinations, make up the bulk of Maria's wares. Then come the almond pastries, the ones for which Maria is best known, in which nuts and sugar blend with surprisingly varied results. A third group of recipes is for the pastries, such as the extremely popular genovesi, made from pasta frolla dough.

Next are recipes for biscuits, from the rather plain and very dry biscuits that Sicilians like to dunk in their morning cappuccino or in a glass of Marsala wine to the richer fig and almond cookies. There is a group of jams and preserves, some cordials, and then a final miscellaneous group that ends with the only – despite its name – savoury dish, polpette dolci.

Since one of our principal motives for working together to create this book has been that of making a historical record, personal opinions and enthusiasms have not played a part in selecting or editing the recipes, and every attempt has been made to be as faithful as possible to the originals. When it has seemed necessary to make substitutions or additions, these are given as optional.

A Note about Almonds

One of the major problems in adapting these recipes is that almonds grown elsewhere lack the intense flavour of Sicilian almonds. We therefore suggest that you compensate when using almonds from other countries by adding a little almond extract, as listed in the recipes. The essential oil evaporates quickly once almonds are ground, causing them to dry out and lose their flavour, so it is important to buy whole almonds, blanched or not, and grind them yourself just before using. A few suggestions for handling almonds follow.

To Blanch Almonds
In the microwave: spread 225 g almonds in a 23-cm glass pie dish or other microwave-safe container, cover with water, and cover with cling film. Microwave on high (100%) for 3 to 4 minutes. Drain, rub the nuts with a kitchen towel, and pop off the skins.

On the stove: place the almonds in a pan and cover with cold water. Bring to a boil, remove from the heat, and drain. Rub the nuts with a kitchen towel and pop off the skins.

TO TOAST ALMONDS

In the microwave: spread 225 g almonds in a 23-cm glass flan dish or other microwave-safe container and microwave on high (100%) for about 6 minutes, turning the dish around once. Cool thoroughly before grinding.

In the oven: spread the nuts on a baking tray and toast in a 180°C/350°F/Gas Mark 4 oven for 10 minutes. Cool thoroughly before grinding.

TO GRIND ALMONDS

Blanched or unblanched almonds can be ground in a nut grinder, meat grinder, or food processor. Always add at least some of the sugar or flour from the recipe to keep the almonds from turning into nut butter.

A Note about Bicarbonate of Ammonia

Many Sicilian biscuit and cookie doughs are leavened with bicarbonate of ammonia, a highly volatile and rather smelly white powder that produces a drier biscuit than any other leavening can, but if overused it will leave a lingering taste of ammonia very foreign to most palates. It is difficult to find bicarbonate of ammonia in the UK, but you can substitute a mixture of baking powder and bicarbonate of soda as suggested in the recipes.

1. Pasta di Mandorla
ALMOND PASTE OR MARZIPAN

*Sugar first came to Europe through Sicily. When the Arabs occu-
pied the island in the ninth century, they introduced the cultivation
of sugarcane, and in the following centuries their confectionery –
comfits, candied fruits, quince and almond pastes – became
extremely popular with the European nobility. Throughout the
Middle Ages and the Renaissance, Sicily exported almond paste,
which was a luxury item conferring great status (in the fourteenth
century a marzipan torte cost more than a brace of peacocks!), and
the island remains famous to this day for its production.*

In making marzipan, or pasta reale *as it is also called, it is
important to grind the almonds yourself, rather than using pre-
ground almond flour, which dries out quickly and loses its essential
oils. Maria describes making almond paste at the San Carlo by
cooking a syrup of water and sugar and then adding the ground
almonds, a complicated process that was necessary because all
but the preliminary grinding had to be done by hand. The advent
of food processors and electric mixers has simplified things
considerably.*

300 g whole blanched almonds
400 g granulated sugar
75 ml water
¼ teaspoon vanilla extract
I teaspoon almond extract (optional)
Icing sugar for dusting

In a meat grinder or a food processor, grind the almonds with about 2 tablespoons of the sugar until very fine, almost powdery.

In a food processor or in an electric mixer, combine the nuts, the rest of the sugar, the water, vanilla and the almond extract, if using. Process or mix until the paste is very smooth. Remove to a marble slab or other cold work surface dusted with icing sugar and knead briefly by hand. Wrap in cling film and refrigerate until ready to use. Marzipan will keep almost indefinitely in the refrigerator.

THIS MAKES 800 G MARZIPAN

2. Pasta per Dolcini
ALMOND PASTRY DOUGH

This is the San Carlo's basic dough for almond pastries that are baked. It is used as is for sospiri, désirs, and cuscinetti, and with slight alterations for belli e brutti. The bocconcini dough is slightly different, in that conserva di cedro replaces the honey and some of the sugar.

Most modern kitchens are equipped with food processors, but I urge you to grind the almonds with a hand-cranked meat grinder if you have one; it will give the almonds a more even texture.

450 g whole blanched almonds
450 g sugar
3 egg whites
I tablespoon honey
I teaspoon almond extract (optional)
I½ teaspoons grated lemon zest

Combine the almonds and sugar in a food processor and grind until medium-fine (do this in batches if the machine is small). Transfer to the large bowl of an electric mixer and add the egg whites, honey, almond extract, if using, and lemon zest. (Or grind the almonds with some of the sugar in a meat grinder, using the fine disc. Transfer to the mixer bowl and add the remaining sugar, the egg whites, honey, almond extract, if using, and lemon zest.)

Using the paddle attachment, beat on low speed until a smooth dough forms and masses around the paddle. Remove and knead briefly to form a ball. Wrap in cling film until ready to use. The dough can be refrigerated for up to 3 days. Bring to room temperature before using.

THIS YIELDS FROM 30 TO 50 PASTRIES
(see individual recipes)

3. Pasta Frolla
BASIC PASTRY DOUGH

Pasta frolla, one of Italy's fundamental pastry doughs, comes in differing degrees of richness. Maria has achieved a very happy medium, which lends itself to both genovesi and crostate with excellent results. Like many Italian pastry chefs, she puts no salt in her doughs and batters; foreign palates may require a little.

250 g durum wheat flour
250 g plain flour
½ teaspoon salt (optional)
200 g sugar
200 g margarine, cut into pieces
4 egg yolks
70 ml cold water, plus more if needed

Process the durum wheat flour in a food processor until fine and silky to the touch, about 5 minutes.

To make the dough in a food processor: add the plain flour, salt, if using, and sugar to the durum wheat flour and pulse to mix. Add the margarine and process until crumbly. Add the egg yolks, one by one, pulsing to mix. With the processor running, add just enough water so the dough comes away from the sides of the bowl. Do not add too much water, or the dough will be difficult to work. Turn out onto a floured surface and form into a ball. Wrap in greaseproof paper or cling film and refrigerate for at least 30 minutes before rolling out.

To make the dough by hand: combine the durum wheat and plain flours, salt, if using, and sugar in a large mixing bowl. Cut in the margarine, using a pastry blender or two knives. Work in the egg yolks, one at a time. Add just enough water so the dough starts to stick together. Turn out onto a floured surface and press the dough together to form a ball. Do not overwork, or the pastry will be tough. Wrap in greaseproof paper or cling film and refrigerate for at least 30 minutes before rolling out.

The dough can be refrigerated for up to 1 week or frozen for up to 1 month.

THIS MAKES ENOUGH FOR TWO 23-CM TARTS OR ONE 37 X 25-CM TART

4. Pan di Spagna
BASIC SPONGE CAKE

Pan di Spagna – 'Spanish bread' – is another fundamental in Italian baking. Meant as a support rather than as a cake in itself, it is rather dry and uninteresting until it gets fancied up with creams and liqueurs. The nuns at the San Carlo called a layer of pan di Spagna a panettone, which literally means 'big loaf' (I doubt they even knew about the brioche-like Northern Italian Christmas bread, rich in raisins and candied fruit, which the world now considers to be panettone). They did lovely things with theirs, like slathering it with jam and almond paste to make torta paradiso.

9 eggs, at room temperature
200 g sugar
½ teaspoon vanilla extract
200 g plain flour

Preheat the oven to 175°C/350°F/Gas Mark 4. Butter two 23-cm tins. Cut a piece of baking parchment or greaseproof paper to fit the bottom of each tin, put it in, and butter it.

Beat the eggs in a bowl for 2 minutes, or until well blended. Add the sugar and beat for 15 to 20 minutes, until very light and fluffy; a ribbon should form when you lift the beater from the bowl. Stir in the vanilla. Sift about a third of the flour over the top and fold in by hand. Continue with the remaining flour until all is incorporated. Pour into the prepared cake tins.

Bake for 25 to 30 minutes or until the tops are golden brown and springy to the touch. A cocktail stick inserted near the centre should come out clean. (Reverse the position of the cake tins after 12 minutes.) Cool in the tins on a rack for 5 minutes, or until the sides of the cakes shrink from the tins. Invert the cakes onto another rack, lift off the tins, and peel off the paper. Turn right side up and cool thoroughly on racks.

If not using immediately, double-wrap each cake in greaseproof paper or cling film and refrigerate for up to 1 week. The cakes can also be wrapped in greaseproof paper or cling film and then in aluminium foil and frozen for up to 1 month.

THIS MAKES TWO 23-CM CAKES

5. Crema Pasticciera
BASIC PASTRY CREAM

This simple and delicate cream, similar to an egg custard, serves as the filling in the genovesi: Maria also fills tarts with it. I would normally cook something like this in a double saucepan, but such things are rare in Sicily, and in fact it seems to work better using direct heat.

2 egg yolks
150 g sugar
40 g cornflour
½ ltr milk
Grated zest of ½ lemon (1¼ teaspoons)

Whisk together the egg yolks and sugar in a small heavy saucepan. Dissolve the cornflour in a quarter of the milk, then gradually add the rest of the milk and mix well. Slowly pour the milk mixture into the egg mixture, whisking until well blended. Place over low heat and cook for 10 to 12 minutes, stirring constantly, until shiny and very thick, the consistency of pudding. (Or cook in a double saucepan for 20 to 25 minutes.) Stir in the lemon zest.

Pour into a bowl and cover with cling film placed directly on top of the cream. Cool and refrigerate until ready to use.

The cream can be refrigerated for up to 3 days. Whisk until smooth if it separates.

THIS MAKES ABOUT 450 ML PASTRY CREAM

6. Crema di Ricotta
RICOTTA CREAM

Ricotta cream incarnates the very essence of the Sicilian sweet tooth, and it is used to fill the humble cassatedde, the world-famous cannoli, and the sumptuous and rather baroque cassata siciliana. Made from sheep's milk and lightly salted even when fresh, Sicilian ricotta is difficult to duplicate elsewhere, but this recipe will give you an acceptable substitute.

450 g full-fat ricotta
130 g sugar
1 teaspoon vanilla extract
¼ teaspoon salt, or to taste

Spoon the ricotta into a strainer lined with muslin or with a paper coffee filter. Set over a bowl, cover, and refrigerate overnight to drain.

Pass the ricotta through a food mill – or beat it gently with an electric mixer or process it briefly in a food processor – to lighten it. Beat in the sugar, vanilla, and salt. Refrigerate or freeze until ready to use. It will keep 3 days in the refrigerator, 1 month in the freezer.

THIS MAKES 450 ML RICOTTA CREAM

7. Frutta di Martorana

MARZIPAN FRUIT

Legend has it that the practice of moulding marzipan into the shape of fruit and painting it was invented by the Mother Superior of the Convent of the Martorana in Palermo, who ordered her nuns to hang the fruit on the trees growing in the cloister as a pleasant surprise for the Archbishop when he came on his paschal visit. Tradition requires that it be made in November, for I Morti, All Souls' Day, when Sicilian children find baskets of marzipan fruit, nuts, and pomegranates at the foot of their beds, left for them by the ghosts of their ancestors. The present-day tourist trade encourages year-round production.

Many Sicilian housewives make their own Martorana for I Morti, just as they make lambs for Easter. Plaster moulds in the form of every imaginable fruit and vegetable are available in Sicily, but with a minimum of dexterity it is possible to make fruit without the moulds.

Cornflour for dusting
Ground cinnamon
1 recipe Pasta di Mandorla (page 118)
**Marzipan or sweet moulds in the shape of fruits and
    vegetables (optional)**
**Vegetable food colouring (red, yellow, blue, and green are
    sufficient)**
**2 or 3 different-sized watercolour or cosmetic brushes,
    including one fine-tipped, and a toothbrush**
Paper or plastic stems and leaves (optional)

Lightly dust your hands and a marble slab or other cold work surface with cornflour that you have flavoured with a very small pinch of ground cinnamon. Take a small piece of marzipan and knead it briefly. Shape it into the form you want if you don't have a mould; small fruits and vegetables are usually the easiest to shape by hand. Or press the kneaded marzipan into a mould and round off the top. Cut away the excess marzipan with a paring knife. Turn the mould over and tap the bottom: the 'fruit' will fall out into your hand. Smooth the seam if necessary.

Shape the remaining marzipan as you like. Set the fruit on a rack to dry overnight.

Pour a few drops of yellow food colouring into a saucer and dilute it with water until very pale yellow. Set aside any strawberries, watermelon slices, mushrooms, and other fruits or vegetables that you intend to colour pink or white. Brush all the rest of the marzipan lightly with the yellow colouring. Use a fairly dry brush: this is merely a base coat that will make the fruit take subsequent colouring more uniformly. Dry for at least 4 hours or overnight.

Mix the colours you want for your marzipan in saucers. Lightly brush each piece until you get the desired effect, always removing excess colouring from the brush before applying it to the marzipan: the idea is to start light and move up, applying the darkest colour last. Remember that no fruit is uniform in colour. Tomatoes often have greenish areas around the stems, apples are green with red and/or yellow overlays, and peaches and apricots usually have pink cheeks.

For spots, speckles, and blemishes, mix a little dark brown colouring by combining red and green and flick it on, using a stiff brush like a toothbrush. Dip the brush in the colouring, hold it near the fruit, and run your finger over the bristles. (It's a good idea to practice on a piece of scrap paper first.)

To make peaches and apricots look fuzzy, after they have

been painted, rub them with a bit of cotton dipped in corn-flour.

While the fruit is still soft, insert stems and leaves, if using. Allow to dry thoroughly. Marzipan will keep indefinitely: for decorative purposes, you can keep it out in the open air (hide a mothball nearby if you have trouble with insects), but if you intend to eat it eventually, it is better stored in an airtight container.

THIS MAKES ABOUT 16 PIECES OF FRUIT OF ASSORTED SIZES

Note: Maria puts a shine on apples, citrus fruits, and so on by coating them with benzoin. Also known as gum benzoin or gum benjamin, this is a resin that comes from Java; it was first brought to the West by a fourteenth-century Arabic voyager, who called it 'incense of Java'. Maria buys it in pieces that look very similar to a violinist's rosin; she pounds it up, and dissolves it in pure alcohol.

8. Belli e Brutti

GOOD AND UGLIES

In central Italy these are known as brutti ma buoni: *'ugly but good'.*
Belli e brutti is Maria's oxymoron, and the translation is my own.

I recipe Pasta per Dolcini (page 120), made with I
 teaspoon baking powder and I teaspoon vanilla
 extract
Icing sugar for dusting

Preheat the oven to 175°C/350°F/Gas Mark 4. Line several baking trays with baking parchment or aluminium foil. If using foil, butter it.

Prepare the dough as described on page 121, adding the baking powder and vanilla to the other ingredients in the mixer bowl. Using a tablespoon, scoop out irregular pieces of dough and put them just as they are, without kneading, on the baking trays about 3 cm apart: they should be rough, spiky mounds.

Bake for 10 to 12 minutes, or until the peaks are golden. Cool briefly on the trays, then transfer to racks. Dust generously with icing sugar then thoroughly cool. Store in an airtight container.

THIS MAKES ABOUT 45 PASTRIES

9. Dolcetti al Liquore
CHOCOLATE-ALMOND TARTLETS

These are the richest, most luscious of the almond pastries. Maria fills them with rum-soaked raisins, but the nuns used Zibibbo grapes, a large and very aromatic variety of table grape, which they had preserved in spirits.

40 g sultanas
400 ml rum
450 g Pasta di Mandorla (page 118)
Cornflour for dusting
60 g dark chocolate
1 teaspoon vegetable oil

Plump the sultanas in a glass of hot water for 1 hour. Drain well. Then soak them in the rum for at least 12 hours.

On a marble slab or other cold work surface, roll out the almond paste ½ cm thick, dusting the surface and the rolling pin with cornflour to prevent sticking. Using a round biscuit cutter, or a glass, cut out twenty-four 5-cm circles. Place 12 circles in small fluted moulds, such as mini-madeleine tins. Fill each tartlet with 1 teaspoon of the sultanas, with a little of the rum, and cover with the remaining circles. Press the edges together with your fingers and cut away the

excess almond paste. Remove the tartlets from the moulds.

Melt the chocolate in a double saucepan or microwave, and stir in the oil. Dip the top half of each tartlet into the chocolate. Set on a rack to harden. Store in an airtight container.

THIS MAKES 12 TARTLETS

Note: If you want to follow the nuns' example, you will need a bunch of large and well-flavoured grapes, such as Muscat. Remove only the grapes that are in perfect condition, taking care to leave the little stems on (the stems allow the grapes to keep better during preserving), wash and dry them, and put them in a jar. Cover with brandy, close tightly, and let stand for at least 6 weeks. When ready to use the grapes, remove them from the alcohol, take off the stems, peel and seed them. Put 1 grape in each tartlet.

10. Sospiri e Désirs
SIGHS AND DESIRES

It is hard to imagine why the nuns gave a French name, désir, to one, and only one, of their pastries. Maria has followed in their footsteps with some uncertainty: sometimes I have seen them labelled in the shop as 'desserts', which I suspect to be the correct name, and at other times as 'désirs', which I much prefer, since I can't resist the languid sound of these in English: sighs and desires.

Granulated sugar for sprinkling
1 recipe Pasta per Dolcini (page 120)
Icing sugar for dusting
About 20 whole blanched almonds

Preheat the oven to 190°C/375°F/Gas Mark 5. Line several baking trays with baking parchment or aluminium foil. If using foil, butter it well.

Sprinkle the work surface with granulated sugar. Set aside a ball of dough about 5 cm in diameter. Divide the remainder into 4 portions. Knead each portion of dough briefly, then roll it under your hands into a long rope about 2 cm thick. Cut it into 3-cm pieces and roll each one between the palms of your hands into a ball. Roll each ball in sugar and flatten slightly into a patty.

To make the sospiri, place half the patties 2 cm apart on the baking trays. Bake for about 12 minutes, or until golden. Cool briefly on the pans, then transfer to racks. While still warm, dust generously with icing sugar.

To make the désirs, place the remaining patties on the baking trays. Work a little water, a few drops at a time, into the reserved dough until it is loose enough to squeeze easily through a pastry bag. Fit the bag with a 1-cm open star and fill it with the dough. Squeeze a small swirl of dough on top of each patty, and top with an almond. Bake for 12 minutes, or until golden. Cool briefly on the pans, then transfer to racks to cool completely.

Store the sospiri and désirs in an airtight container.

THIS MAKES ABOUT 40 PASTRIES

11. Cuscinetti
ALMOND PILLOWS

These are filled pastries that use the same almond pastry dough as the sospiri and désirs: thus, if you make up a big batch of dough, you can make assorted pastries with very little work – several pigeons with one fava bean, as the Italians would say.

Sugar for sprinkling
1 recipe Pasta per Dolcini (page 120)
340 g Conserva di Cedro (page 188)

Preheat the oven to 190°C/375°F/Gas Mark 5. Line several baking trays with baking parchment or aluminium foil. If using foil, butter it well.

Sprinkle the work surface and rolling pin with sugar. Divide the dough into 4 portions. Roll each portion into a rectangle about 25 x 10 x ½ cm thick. Place a strip of conserva down the length of each rectangle and fold the sides of the pastry over tightly to make a sausage. Roll each sausage back and forth with the palms of your hands until it is about 40 cm and about 2 cm in diameter. Flatten slightly and cut on a slight diagonal into 3-cm pieces. Place cut side up 2 cm apart on the baking trays.

Bake for 15 minutes, or until golden brown. Cool the pastries briefly on the pan on a rack, then transfer to racks to cool. Store in an airtight container.

THIS MAKES 48 PASTRIES

Variation: These may be made also with Marmellata di Limone (page 190). They should be baked at a lower temperature, 175°C/350°F/Gas Mark 4, for 10 to 12 minutes.

12. Bocconcini
ALMOND BITES

*In the bocconcini made by the nuns of the San Carlo the citron
preserves were blended together with the ground almonds; the nuns
at the Badia Grande in my husband's hometown of Alcamo stuck
the preserves in the centre as a filling. I can remember my mother-
in-law sending large bags of almonds from the family farm to the
Badia, where they were transformed into absolutely delicious
bocconcini baked in a wood oven. The nuns at the Badia are still
going strong and they still make bocconcini to give as presents, but
they stopped making them for sale when the Italian government
introduced VAT and bookkeeping became too complicated.*

450 g whole blanched almonds
350 g sugar, plus sugar for sprinkling
340 g Conserva di Cedro (page 188)
1 teaspoon almond extract (optional)
1 to 2 tablespoons water

Preheat the oven to 190°C/375°F/Gas Mark 5. Line several
baking trays with baking parchment or aluminium foil. If
using foil, butter and flour it.

Combine the almonds and the sugar in a food processor
and grind until medium-fine. Add the conserva and almond

extract, if using, and process until combined. Do this in batches if the machine is small. The mixture will look crumbly. Add up to a tablespoonful of water, a little at a time, until the dough just begins to stick together. (Or grind the almonds with some of the sugar in a meat grinder using the fine disc. Transfer to the large bowl of an electric mixer and add the remaining sugar, the conserva, and almond extract, if using. Using the paddle attachment, mix until combined, adding just enough water so the dough starts to stick together.)

Sprinkle the work surface with sugar. Transfer the dough to the surface and knead and work it together. Divide the dough into 4 portions. Form each portion into a log about 4 cm thick, and slice into 2-cm pieces. Knead each piece briefly and then roll it between your hands into a ball. Roll it in sugar and flatten slightly into a patty. Place the patties 2 cm apart on the baking trays.

Bake for 15 minutes, or until golden. Cool briefly on the pans, then transfer to racks to cool thoroughly. Store in an airtight container.

THIS MAKES ABOUT 30 PASTRIES

13. Palline all'Arancia
ORANGE BALLS

The ever-frugal nuns would save the peels from Marmellata di Arance II (page 200), coat them heavily with sugar to keep them from spoiling, and then use them instead of whole oranges to make these pastries. Maria occasionally does the same herself, but she says they are better if made with the whole orange.

200 g whole blanched almonds
200 g sugar, plus sugar for sprinkling and coating
½ medium navel orange, unpeeled (scrub before processing)
1 tablespoon rum
1 teaspoon almond extract (optional)

Combine the almonds, the sugar, and orange in a food processor and process until the almonds are ground medium-fine. Transfer the mixture to a bowl and stir in the rum and almond extract.

Sprinkle the work surface with sugar. Knead the dough briefly on the sugar and divide it in half. Roll each piece of dough on the sugar into a log about 3 cm in diameter.

Cut each log into ½-cm pieces. Dip the cut sides in sugar, roll the pieces into balls, coat with sugar, then let dry 3 hours.

Put the balls in paper cases in an airtight container. Let them sit 3 to 4 days before serving. They will keep for weeks.

THIS MAKES ABOUT TWENTY-FOUR 3-CM BALLS

14. Palline al Cioccolato
CHOCOLATE BALLS

A variation on the preceding recipe, this is one of the very few pastries in which the nuns used chocolate.

200 g whole blanched almonds
200 g sugar, plus sugar for sprinkling and coating
3 tablespoons cocoa powder
1 tablespoon rum
1 teaspoon almond extract (optional)
4 teaspoons water

Combine the almonds, sugar, and cocoa in a food processor and process until the almonds are ground medium-fine. Transfer the mixture to a bowl and stir in the rum and almond extract, if using. Stir in the water, a teaspoon at a time, to make a stiff dough.

Sprinkle the work surface with sugar. Knead the dough briefly on the sugar and divide it in half. Roll each piece of dough into a log about 3 cm in diameter.

Slice each log into 3-cm pieces. Dip the cut sides of each piece in sugar, then roll in your hands into a ball. Coat each ball with sugar. Place the balls on a tray and let dry for 3 hours.

Place each ball in a paper case and transfer the balls to an airtight container. Let mellow for 3 to 4 days before serving.

The balls will keep for weeks in an airtight container.

THIS MAKES ABOUT TWENTY-FOUR 3-CM BALLS

15. Lingue di Suocera
MOTHER-IN-LAW'S TONGUES

This recipe opens the section dealing with pasta frolla, but it has one foot in the preceding section, since, despite their name, mother-in-law's tongues are small and sweet, and they are sold and served as assorted tea cakes together with all the little almond pastries.

½ recipe Pasta Frolla (page 122)
About 225 ml Conserva di Cedro (page 188) or
  Marmellata di Limone (page 190)
Icing sugar for dusting

Preheat the oven to 190°C/375°F/Gas Mark 5. Line several baking trays with baking parchment or foil. If using foil, butter and flour it.

On a floured surface roll out the dough to a little less than ½ cm thick. With a 9 x 5 cm fluted oval biscuit cutter, cut out ovals of dough. (If you do not have a biscuit cutter, make a template and cut out ovals, or rectangles, of the same size with a pastry cutter.) Press the scraps together into a ball, roll out, and cut out another 3 or 4 ovals.

Wet your fingers with water, and shape about 2 teaspoons of the preserves into a 7-cm roll. Place it down the centre of an oval of dough. Fold together the sides until they almost touch, and pinch the ends. Repeat with the rest of the ovals, and place about 2 cm apart on the baking trays.

Bake for 15 to 20 minutes, or until golden. Transfer to racks to cool. While still warm, dust with icing sugar. Store in an airtight container.

THIS MAKES ABOUT 24 PASTRIES

16. Genovesi
GENOA CAKES

These are perhaps the hottest-selling item in Maria's shop: many locals pass by daily to get one still warm from the oven to eat on the spot. In form at least, they are a version of what are known in Palermo as minni di virgini *– 'virgin's breasts' – an allusion both to their rounded shape and to the nuns of the Monastero delle Vergini, who made them. In Catania they put a cherry on top and call them* minni di Sant'Agata *in honour of that city's patron saint, who, to symbolize her martyrdom, is usually depicted holding her severed breasts on a plate.*

½ recipe Pasta Frolla (page 122)
½ recipe Crema Pasticciera (page 126)
Icing sugar for dusting

Preheat the oven to 220°C/425°F/Gas Mark 7.

Divide the dough into 8 pieces. On a floured surface, roll out each piece into a rectangle about 15 x 10 x ½ cm thick.

Place 2 tablespoons of the cream on one half of each rectangle, fold the other half over, and press the edges together with your fingers. Then cut out circles from the rectangles, using a 7-cm round fluted biscuit cutter, a drinking glass, or a pastry wheel, and place about 2 cm apart on a baking tray.

Bake for 7 minutes, or until lightly browned. Transfer to a rack to cool briefly. Sprinkle with icing sugar. Genovesi are best eaten warm.

THIS MAKES 8 CAKES

17. Panzarotti
BAKED RICOTTA TURNOVERS

Panzarotti – *'little bellies'* – owe their name to their half-moon shape, which, together with their ricotta cream filling, is what distinguishes them from genovesi. The ingredients and the procedures are almost the same, so if you were to make them simultaneously, you would save time and multiply delight.

½ recipe Pasta Frolla (page 122)
½ recipe Crema di Ricotta (page 128)
Icing sugar for dusting

Preheat the oven to 220°C/425°F/Gas Mark 7.

Divide the dough into 7 pieces. On a floured surface, roll out each piece into a rectangle about 15 x 10 x 1 cm thick. (The rectangle should be a little thicker than for genovesi because the filling is runnier.)

Place 2 heaped tablespoons of the ricotta cream on one half of each rectangle, close to the centre. Fold the dough over and seal. Using a pastry wheel or a fluted round biscuit cutter placed off-centre, cut each pastry into a half-moon shape, leaving the folded side intact, as in a turnover. Place about 2 cm apart on a baking tray.

Bake for 8 minutes, or until lightly browned. Remove to a rack. Sprinkle with icing sugar, and serve warm.

THIS MAKES 7 TURNOVERS

18. Crostata di Marmellata
JAM TART

At the San Carlo, tarts were made to order, so you could choose a cream, ricotta, or jam filling. Peach jam was the most common, simply because all the jams were homemade and peaches were cheap. Occasionally someone would make the nuns a present of quinces, and then there would be quince paste and quince jam, which makes a delicious and unusual tart.

½ recipe Pasta Frolla (page 122)
400 ml Marmellata di Cotogne (page 192), Marmellata di Pesche (page 197), or Marmellata di Arance II (page 200)

Preheat the oven to 190°C/375°F/Gas Mark 5. Butter and flour a 23-cm pie dish or flan tin.

Divide the dough into 2 pieces, one slightly larger than the other. Put the smaller piece back in the refrigerator. Roll out the larger piece into a circle large enough to line the bottom and sides of the pie dish or flan tin with a 2-cm overhang, and place the dough in the pan. Spread the marmellata evenly over the bottom. Break off pieces of the refrigerated dough and roll them under your hands into a dozen long, thin 'snakes'. Arrange these on the top of the tart in a lattice pattern. Trim the ends even with the edge of the dish or tin, bring the overhang of dough up and over the ends, and crimp. (You will have some dough left over. Refrigerate for another purpose.)

Bake for 20 to 25 minutes, or until the pastry is golden brown. Let cool before serving.

THIS MAKES ONE 23-CM PIE OR TART

Note: The nuns used to make a rather flavourless jelly from the water in which they had cooked the quinces for *cotognata*, which they then spooned onto the quince jam in the crostata to give it a shine. Maria still does this but claims there is no point in doing so for home bakers. There is little or no visible difference.

19. Crostata di Ricotta

RICOTTA TART

Maria sells all of her crostate either whole or by the slice, and as individual tartlets as well. This one is known elsewhere as cassata al forno – *'baked cassata' – to distinguish it from the more elegant and better-known* cassata siciliana, *which is sponge cake filled with ricotta cream and covered with almond paste and icing, then topped with candied fruit.*

½ **recipe Pasta Frolla (page 122)**
1½ **times the recipe Crema di Ricotta (page 128)**

Preheat the oven to 190°C/375°F/Gas Mark 5. Butter and flour a 23-cm pie dish or flan tin. (Or you can use individual tins.)

Divide the dough into 2 pieces, one slightly larger than the other, and put the smaller piece back in the refrigerator. Roll out the larger piece as directed on page 156 and fit it into the pie dish. Fill with the ricotta cream, and top with lattice strips as on page 157.

Bake 25 to 30 minutes (about 20 minutes for tartlets), or until the pastry is golden brown. Let cool before serving.

THIS MAKES ONE 23-CM PIE OR TART OR EIGHT 9-CM TARTLETS

20. Crostata di Crema

CUSTARD TART

Maria makes two versions of this tart: one covered with a pastry lattice like that of the Crostata di Marmellata, and a richer one, in which she replaces the lattice with a heavy sprinkling of almonds or pine nuts. She uses whole almonds for this, but flaked almonds might sit more lightly on such a delicate filling.

½ recipe Pasta Frolla (page 122)
1 ½ times the recipe Crema Pasticciera (page 126)

Preheat the oven to 190°C/375°F/Gas Mark 5. Butter and flour a 23-cm pie dish.

Divide the dough into 2 pieces, one slightly larger than the other. Put the smaller piece back in the refrigerator. Roll out the larger piece into a circle large enough to line the bottom and sides with a 2-cm overhang, and place the dough in the dish. Fill with the crema and smooth the top. Break off pieces of the refrigerated dough and roll them under your hands into a dozen long, thin 'snakes'. Arrange these on the top of the tart in a lattice pattern. Trim the ends even with the edge of the dish, bring the overhang of dough up and over the ends, and crimp. (You will have some leftover dough. Refrigerate for another purpose.)

Bake for 20 to 25 minutes, or until the pastry is golden brown. Let cool before serving.

THIS MAKES ONE 23-CM PIE OR TART

Variation: For a fancier version, omit the lattice topping and arrange 120 g whole blanched almonds on top, or sprinkle with 50 g pine nuts. (You will need about ⅓ recipe Pasta Frolla.) Flute the edge of the pastry.

21. Crostata di Frutta

FRESH FRUIT TART

Fresh fruit had little place in the San Carlo pantry except at jam-making time: this is a late addition to Maria's repertoire.

½ recipe **Pasta Frolla (page 122)**
½–⅓ recipe **Crema Pasticciera (page 126) or 60 g apricot
  or other fruit jelly, melted**
**Slices of fresh fruit, such as peaches, nectarines, pears,
  and kiwis, or tangerine sections, berries, or grapes**
60 g apricot jelly, melted

Preheat the oven to 220°C/425°F/Gas Mark 7. Butter and flour a 23-cm pie dish.

Roll out the dough into a 32-cm circle. Line the bottom and sides of the pan with it, and flute the edge. Prick the bottom of the pie shell. Bake for 15 minutes, or until golden brown. Let cool on a rack before filling.

Spread the bottom of the shell with a ½-cm layer of pastry cream, or paint it with 60 g melted apricot jelly. Arrange the fruit on top in a decorative pattern. Using a pastry brush, paint the fruit with the second batch of melted jelly. Serve.

THIS MAKES ONE 23-CM PIE OR TART

Note: Melt jelly for tarts in a small saucepan or in the microwave on high (100% power) for 1 minute. Strain. Leftover jelly will keep indefinitely in a covered jar in the refrigerator. Reheat before using.

22. Biscotti al Fico

FIG BISCUITS

Fig-filled biscuits like these are made all over Sicily at Christmas-time, but are known by different names, such as cudduredde, nucatoli, *and* bucellatini. *Sicilian women are very skilled at varying the way they shape and slit these pastries, twisting them into a whole range of sensuous baroque forms.*

PASTRY

250 g durum wheat flour
250 g plain flour
200 g sugar
2 teaspoons bicarbonate of ammonia or 2 teaspoons
    baking powder plus 2 teaspoons bicarbonate of soda
225 g margarine, cut into pieces
1 teaspoon vanilla extract
125 ml milk

FILLING

450 g dried figs
½ small orange, unpeeled (scrub before cutting)
60 g sugar
50 g whole blanched almonds or walnuts, roughly
    chopped
⅛ teaspoon ground cloves
1 teaspoon ground cinnamon
2 tablespoons honey
Hundreds and Thousands (optional)

To make the pastry, process the durum wheat flour in a food processor until fine and silky to the touch, about 5 minutes.

Combine the durum wheat and the plain flours, the sugar, and bicarbonate of ammonia in a large mixing bowl. Cut in the margarine, using a pastry blender or two knives. Stir the vanilla extract into the milk, and add just enough of the milk to make the dough stick together; do not make it too wet, or it will be hard to work. Press the dough together into a ball, working it as little as possible. Wrap in greaseproof paper or cling film and refrigerate for at least 30 minutes. (The dough can also be made in a food processor, following the directions for Pasta Frolla on page 122.)

To make the filling, grind the figs in a meat grinder fitted with the small blade. Cut the orange into pieces, remove the seeds, and grind it.

Place the figs and orange in a large bowl, or the large bowl of an electric mixer, and add the sugar, nuts, cloves, and cinnamon. Using a wooden spoon, or the paddle attachment of the mixer, mix well. Add the honey and mix well. (The filling can be refrigerated for up to 1 week or frozen for 1 month.)

Preheat the oven to 190°C/375°F/Gas Mark 5. Line several baking trays with baking parchment or aluminium foil. If using foil, grease it.

Divide the dough into 6 portions. Roll each piece into a rectangle about 23 cm long, 10 to 12 cm wide, and ½ cm thick. Place a strip of filling down one side, fold the dough over, and seal the edges. Cut each roll into 3 pieces. With a sharp knife, make several 2-cm cuts in the folded side of each pastry, then bend it into a crescent, with the slits on the outside so that the slits open slightly to show the dark filling.

Place the pastries about 3 cm apart on the baking trays, and sprinkle with Hundreds and Thousands if you wish.

Bake for about 25 minutes or until very lightly browned. Cool on racks. Store in an airtight container.

THIS MAKES **18** PASTRIES

23. Mostaccioli di Erice

ERICE CINNAMON BISCUITS

San Carlo was famous above all for its production of mostaccioli (mustazzoli *in Sicilian), very dry, hard biscuits seasoned with cinnamon and cloves, most often served with a dessert wine into which they could be dipped to soften them. Before baking, the biscuits are rolled between ridged wooden paddles, similar to the ones we use for making butter balls, known as* pettine – *'combs' – which impress a criss-cross pattern on them. This procedure requires both the paddles and considerable skill. A similar effect can be achieved with a sharp knife.*

Mostaccioli will keep up to six months in a well-closed container; at the San Carlo they were kept in big wooden chests with domed tops. The peculiar quantities called for in this recipe are the equivalents of ancient measures such as the munedda.

220 g sugar
2 packed teaspoons bicarbonate of ammonia or 2 packed teaspoons baking powder plus 2 packed teaspoons bicarbonate of soda
150 ml water
360 g durum wheat flour
20 g whole blanched almonds, lightly toasted
180 g plain flour
1¼ teaspoons ground cloves
2¼ teaspoons ground cinnamon

Put the sugar in a glass bowl, add the ammonia, and stir in the water. Mix well. Let stand for 2 to 3 hours, or until the sugar is completely dissolved.

Preheat the oven to 220°C/425°F/Gas Mark 7. Line 2 baking trays with baking parchment or aluminium foil. If using foil, grease it.

Process the durum wheat flour in a food processor until fine and silky to the touch, about 5 minutes.

Grind the almonds with a tablespoon of the plain flour, using a meat grinder or a food processor, as on page 117.

In a bowl, combine the remaining plain and the durum wheat flours, the spices, and almonds, and mix well. Make a well in the centre and add the dissolved sugar. Swish 60 ml water around the sides of the bowl to pick up any remaining sugar crystals and add that as well. Mix with a wooden spoon or the paddle attachment of a mixer until just combined.

Turn out onto a floured surface and knead very briefly. Break off pieces the size of a lime and roll each one between your floured hands into a sausage about 10 cm long and 2 cm in diameter. Flatten each one slightly and score with a knife in a crisscross pattern.

Place 3 cm apart on baking trays and bake until the biscuits begin to brown, about 20 minutes. To dry further, crowd all the biscuits on one ungreased baking tray and leave in the turned-off oven until cool. Remove and completely cool on racks. Store in an airtight container.

THIS MAKES ABOUT 24 BISCUITS

Note: If you substitute 2 teaspoons baking powder plus 2 teaspoons bicarbonate of soda for the bicarbonate of ammonia, do not add them to the water and sugar, but to the flours, spices, and almonds.

24. Biscotti al Latte

MILK BISCUITS

This is the biscuit that Titì made Maria put back! They are dry and rather uninteresting, hardly worth a good cry in an affluent world, but are nonetheless very popular with Sicilians, who dip them in their breakfast cappuccino.

250 g durum wheat flour
250 g plain flour
150 g sugar
1 packed tablespoon bicarbonate of ammonia (or 1
    tablespoon baking powder plus 1 tablespoon
    bicarbonate of soda)
100 g margarine
1 teaspoon vanilla extract
125 ml warm milk

Process the durum wheat flour in a food processor until fine and silky to the touch, about 5 minutes.

Combine the durum and plain flours, the sugar, and bicarbonate of ammonia in a large mixing bowl. Cut in the margarine, using a pastry blender or two knives. Stir the vanilla extract into the milk, and add just enough milk to make the dough stick together. Press together to make a ball;

do not overwork. Wrap in greaseproof paper or cling film and refrigerate for at least 30 minutes. (The dough can also be made in a food processor, following the directions for Pasta Frolla on page 122.)

Preheat the oven to 190°C/375°F/Gas Mark 5. Line 2 baking trays with baking parchment or aluminium foil. If using foil, grease it.

Turn the dough out onto a floured surface and knead very briefly. Break off pieces the size of a lime and roll each piece between your floured hands into a sausage about 10 cm long and 2 cm in diameter. Flatten slightly and place 3 cm apart on the baking trays.

Bake for 25 minutes, or until lightly browned. Turn off the oven and leave the biscuits in it until it is cool. Cool the biscuits thoroughly on racks. Store in an airtight container.

THIS MAKES ABOUT 20 BISCUITS

25. Biscotti all'Anice

ANISEED BISCUITS

These biscuits are made in summertime, since they are considered the ideal accompaniment to granita di limone.

3 eggs 170 g sugar
¹/₃ teaspoon vanilla extract
¹/₂ teaspoon bicarbonate of ammonia (or ¹/₂ teaspoon
**   baking powder plus ¹/₂ teaspoon bicarbonate of soda)**
250 g plain flour
1 tablespoon plus 1 teaspoon aniseeds

Preheat the oven to 190°C/375°F/Gas Mark 5. Line several baking trays with baking parchment or foil. If using foil, grease it.

Beat the eggs lightly in a large mixing bowl. Add the sugar and vanilla. With a whisk, beat until light and fluffy and a ribbon begins to form when the whisk is lifted from the bowl, about 8 minutes.

Mix the bicarbonate of ammonia and flour. Stir one quarter of the flour mixture into the egg mixture. Fold in the rest of the flour in three additions. Fold in the aniseeds.

Put the batter in a piping bag fitted with a large plain nozzle (or use a large spoon), pipe (or spoon) the batter onto the baking trays, forming loaves about 6 to 7 cm long, and about 5 cm wide.

Bake for about 20 to 25 minutes, or until golden. Remove from the oven and turn the temperature down to 150°C/300°F/Gas Mark 2.

Cool the loaves briefly on the trays. Then transfer to a cutting board, and cut on the diagonal into slices 1 to 2 cm thick. Lay on an ungreased baking tray and bake, turning once, until very lightly toasted, about 5 minutes on each side. Cool thoroughly on racks. Store in an airtight container.

THIS MAKES 40 TO 50 BISCUITS

26. Reginette
QUEEN'S BISCUITS

Biscuits rolled in sesame seeds are a great favourite all over the island (Sicilians love sesame and sprinkle the seeds on their bread, too), but the dough can differ greatly. The chef at Regaleali, Mario LoMenzo, makes very fancy reginette, rich in eggs and butter, while country bakeries usually offer much more humble versions. The San Carlo reginette (only slightly different from their milk biscuits) tend towards the latter.

250 g durum wheat flour
250 g plain flour
150 g sugar
2 teaspoons bicarbonate of ammonia (or 2 teaspoons
    baking powder plus 2 teaspoons bicarbonate of soda)
100 g margarine
1 teaspoon vanilla extract
125 ml warm milk
75 g sesame seeds

Process the durum wheat flour in a food processor until fine and silky to the touch, about 5 minutes.

Combine the durum wheat and plain flours, the sugar, and bicarbonate of ammonia in a large mixing bowl. Cut in the margarine, using a pastry blender or two knives. Stir the vanilla extract into the milk, and add just enough milk to make the dough stick together. Press together to make a ball; do not overwork. Wrap in greaseproof paper or cling film and refrigerate for at least 30 minutes. (The dough can also be made in a food processor, following the directions for Pasta Frolla on page 122.)

Preheat the oven to 190°C/375°F/Gas Mark 5. Line several baking trays with baking parchment or aluminium foil. If using foil, grease it.

Divide the dough into 8 portions. Roll each piece under your hands into a 2-cm rope. Cut into 5-cm lengths and roll briefly between your palms to round the ends. Wet the sesame seeds thoroughly with water, drain, and spread out on a plate. Roll each piece of dough in the wet seeds to coat well, and place 2 cm apart on the baking trays.

Bake for 25 minutes, or until lightly browned. Turn off the

oven and leave the biscuits in it until it is cool. Cool the biscuits thoroughly on racks. Store in an airtight container.

THIS MAKES ABOUT 40 BISCUITS

27. Mostaccioli di Vino Cotto

MUST BISCUITS

For All Souls' Day at the beginning of November, the San Carlo nuns made a different kind of mostaccioli, the traditional holiday biscuits that are made all over Sicily and that, as their name indicates, are made with mosto, grape must that has been boiled down into vino cotto, a typical Sicilian sweetener ever since the classical era. Maria's mother used to spice them with black pepper and shape them into dolls and animals, the only toys she could afford to give her children for I Morti. Nardo calls the more prosaic biscuits that the nuns made strunzi ri 'attu ('cat turds'), but he is referring to appearance alone. They taste very good.

2 small oranges
250 g durum wheat flour
250 g plain flour
100 g sugar
1½ teaspoons bicarbonate of ammonia (or 1½ teaspoons
    baking powder plus 1½ teaspoons bicarbonate of
    soda)
½ teaspoon ground cloves
2 teaspoons ground cinnamon
½ teaspoon freshly ground black pepper (optional)
150 g honey or vino cotto (see note)
¼ cup sesame seeds, immersed in water and drained

Preheat the oven to 190°C/375°F/Gas Mark 5. Line several
baking trays with baking parchment or aluminium foil. If
using foil, grease it.

Scrub the oranges, quarter them, and remove any seeds.
Cut into small pieces and grind in a meat grinder, using the
fine blade, or in a food processor.

Process the durum wheat flour in a food processor until
fine and silky to the touch, about 5 minutes.

In a large bowl, or the bowl of an electric mixer, combine

the durum wheat and plain flours, the sugar, bicarbonate of ammonia, cloves, cinnamon, and pepper, if using, and mix well. With a wooden spoon, or the paddle attachment, beat in the ground oranges and the honey or vino cotto. Turn the dough out onto a well-floured surface and knead very briefly. If the oranges are very juicy, you may have to dust the dough with flour. (At this point, the dough can be refrigerated for several hours.)

Divide the dough into 6 portions. Roll each piece under your floured hands into a long rope about 2 cm in diameter. Cut each rope into 5-cm lengths. Dip one end of each one into the wet sesame seeds, and place the biscuits on a baking tray, about 2 cm apart.

Bake for 15 to 20 minutes, or until dark brown. Remove and cool thoroughly on racks. Store in an airtight container.

THIS MAKES 40 TO 45 BISCUITS

Note: You can make vino cotto by taking 900 g of white grapes, removing their stems, and passing them through a food mill. The resulting juice must be clarified, either by bringing it to a boil with 2 tablespoons of wood ash and allowing it to settle overnight, or by filtering it through a paper coffee filter. Bring the clarified juice to a boil and simmer until it is reduced by two thirds. Maria says that if she has no vino cotto she uses double the amount of sugar in the original recipe and adds 2 tablespoons honey and ¼ teaspoon cocoa powder. Honey works beautifully as a substitute for vino cotto.

28. Amaretti
ALMOND COOKIES

My mother-in-law used to make these flat, crisp cookies, which are of a very different nature from the chewy almond pastries. There is a glass jar of amaretti on Maria's counter, and she always sends me home with some for my husband.

300 g whole unblanched almonds, toasted
250 g sugar
25 g plain flour
¼ teaspoon salt (optional)
4 egg whites
2 teaspoons almond extract (optional)

Preheat the oven to 150°C/300°F/Gas Mark 2. Line a baking tray with aluminium foil, and butter and flour it.

Combine the almonds, sugar, flour, and salt, if using, in a food processor. Process to a fine, crumbly powder. Transfer to a bowl and stir in the egg whites and almond extract, if using.

Drop the batter by the teaspoonful onto the baking tray, about 3 cm apart. Bake for 20 minutes, or until dry. Let cool slightly on the baking tray, then transfer to a rack to cool completely.

Store in an airtight container.

THIS MAKES ABOUT 48 COOKIES

29. Quaresimali
LENTEN BISCUITS

One is allowed to eat these biscuits during Quaresima – *the Lenten period of fasting – because they contain neither egg yolks nor fat. (Nor do any of the almond pastries, but that's quibbling – these do seem more austere.) They can be found throughout Italy under different names: in Tuscany, for example, they are called* cantucci.

250 g whole blanched almonds
250 g sugar
2 tablespoons (25 g) plain flour
2 egg whites
½ teaspoon vanilla extract
½ teaspoon almond extract (optional)

Preheat the oven to 200°C/400°F/Gas Mark 6. Line a baking tray with baking parchment, and grease it.

Set aside 50 g of the almonds. Grind the rest of the almonds with about 2 tablespoons of the sugar.

Combine the ground almonds, whole almonds, flour, and the rest of the sugar in a large bowl. Using the paddle or flat beater, mix well. Beat in 1 egg white, then add the vanilla and almond extract, if using. Beat in the second egg white and beat until the dough masses around the paddle. The dough will be very stiff.

Divide the dough in half. Shape it into two 23 x 6 x 3-cm loaves and place on the baking tray. Bake for 20 minutes, or until lightly browned. Reduce the oven temperature to 150°C/300°F/Gas Mark 2, and cool the loaves on a rack.

Cut the loaves on the diagonal into slices about 1 cm thick. Lay the biscuits on an ungreased baking tray and bake for 8 minutes, or until lightly browned on top. Turn the slices over and brown the other side. Remove and cool on racks. Store in an airtight container.

THIS MAKES 34 BISCUITS

30. Conserva di Cedro
CITRON PRESERVES

These preserves were one of the mainstays of the San Carlo pastry making. Citrons are getting harder and harder to find: the demand for them is limited and the citron is one of the most delicate of the citrus trees, so not many are being grown any more. Maria has been forced to turn to industrially produced preserves to ensure the quantity she needs, but the homemade kind is markedly better. If you intend to make marzipan hearts or lambs, you must make your preserves stiff enough to hold their shape firmly when moulded; for use in bocconcini, cuscinetti, and lingue di suocera they need not be quite so dense. A jelly bag, scales, and preserving jars with lids are required.

1.8 kg citrons
1.35 kg sugar

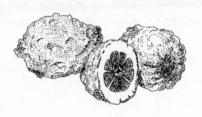

Cut the citrons into pieces and discard the pulp and seeds. Grate the peels (both the yellow zest and all the white pith) or grind in a meat grinder, using the medium blade.

Put the ground peels in a loosely woven jelly bag and close tightly. Wash the peel in the bag, kneading it under running water, until the water runs clear. Allow to stand in a bowl of water, changing the water and wringing the bag out well every day, for 3 to 5 days, or until the peel no longer has a bitter taste.

Wring the bag of peel to squeeze out as much water as possible. Remove the peel from the bag and weigh it. Then put it in a heavy stainless steel, copper, or earthenware saucepan (don't use aluminium, which would cause it to turn black), and add an equal amount by weight of sugar.

Cook over low heat, stirring constantly, until the preserves are very, very dense and come away from the sides of the pan as you stir. Spoon into hot sterilized jars and seal. Store in a cool, dark place for at least 2 months before using.

THIS MAKES FIVE TO SIX 250-ML JARS OF PRESERVES

31. Marmellata di Limone

LEMON MARMALADE

Since citrons are not easy to find in the UK, Maria suggests using this lemon marmalade as a substitute for conserva di cedro in making bocconcini or lingue di suocera. But in order to do so, you must make it much denser than an ordinary marmalade.

1 kg large thick-skinned lemons, preferably organic (about 6 lemons)
1.4 kg sugar

Scrub the lemons and prick them all over with a fork. Put them in a bowl with water to cover and let soak for at least 5 days, changing the water every day.

Drain the lemons, quarter them, and remove the seeds. Cut into small pieces and pass through a meat grinder, using the fine blade. Weigh the pulp and put it in a large non-aluminium saucepan with a little less than 1¼ times its weight in sugar.

Cook over medium-low heat, stirring occasionally, until the jam starts to boil, about 15 minutes. Cook, stirring frequently, until the jam begins to thicken, then stir constantly until the jam is fairly thick, about 30 minutes. To test, drop half a teaspoonful onto a plate: if the marmalade spreads only slightly, it is ready to be put in jars for jam. If you are making the marmalade to use in pastries, cook it 20 to 30 minutes more, until it is very dense: if you drop half a teaspoonful onto a plate and it holds its shape, it is done.

Spoon the jam into hot sterilized jars and seal. Store in a cool, dark place for at least 2 months before using.

THIS MAKES FIVE 250-ML JARS OF MARMALADE

32. Marmellata di Cotogne
QUINCE JAM

Quinces were one of the fruits most frequently used in the Middle Ages and the Renaissance. They have a wonderful, old-fashioned flavour, and deserve to be rediscovered.

1.35 kg quinces (8 small quinces)
2 lemons, sliced
1 kg sugar

Wash the quinces. Put them in a large non-aluminium pot, add the lemons and water to cover, and weight the fruit down with a plate. Cook until the quinces are tender enough to pierce with a fork, about 30 to 45 minutes, depending on the size of the fruit. Remove the quinces from the pot as they are done. Discard the lemons.

When cool enough to handle, cut the quinces into pieces and remove the seeds and cores. Purée the quinces in a food processor or in a meat grinder fitted with the coarse blade. Weigh the purée, and put it in a large saucepan. Add an equal amount by weight of sugar, or slightly less if you prefer your jam less sweet, and stir well.

Cook, uncovered, over medium heat, stirring occasionally, until the jam starts to boil. Cook, stirring frequently, until the mixture begins to thicken, then stir constantly until the jam is thick and looks translucent and shiny.

Spoon the jam into hot sterilized jars and seal. Store in a cool, dark place for at least 1 month before using.

THIS MAKES ABOUT SEVEN 250-ML JARS OF JAM

33. Cotognata
QUINCE PASTE

Very much a delicacy and a status symbol in medieval times when sugar was extremely expensive, quince paste often appeared on fancy banquet menus, and small ceramic dishes with crests or religious symbols on them were (and still are) produced especially for moulding it. It is now considered to be something of a rustic throwback, and has once more become chic for just that reason. The nuns made a little for their own pleasure when someone made them a present of quinces, but Maria makes and sells large quantities every year.

1.35 kg quinces (7 medium quinces)
2 lemons, sliced
800 g to 1 kg sugar, plus extra sugar for coating

Wash the quinces and put them in a large pot. Add the lemons and water to cover, and weight down the fruit. Cook, uncovered, until the quinces are tender enough to pierce with a fork, about 30 minutes. Drain, and discard the lemons.

When the quinces are cool enough to handle, quarter them and remove the seeds and cores. Cut into small pieces. Pass through a food mill, using the medium blade, to make a smooth purée the consistency of apple sauce. Weigh the purée, and measure out an equal weight of sugar, or slightly less if you prefer the paste not too sweet. Set aside.

Lightly coat the inside of a large tin or several smaller moulds with vegetable oil.

Put the purée in a large pot and stir in the sugar. Cook over medium-high heat, stirring occasionally, until the mixture comes to a boil. Cook, stirring occasionally, until the mixture starts to thicken, then reduce the heat to medium and cook, stirring constantly, until the paste is very dense and shiny and comes away from the sides of the pot as you stir, 45 minutes to 1 hour in all.

Transfer to the oiled tin and smooth the top. Cover with a piece of muslin and set aside in a dry place for several days, until the sides of the paste have come away from the sides of the tin(s) and the top feels only slightly tacky. Invert the paste onto a plate to dry the other side. (If you live in a damp climate, place the tin in the oven with just the pilot light on. Let the paste dry for 3 days, then invert and dry on the other side for 1 day.)

If you have used a large tin rather than small moulds, cut the paste into squares. Dip the cotognata in granulated sugar to coat. Wrap loosely in greaseproof paper and store at room temperature, in an open dish or basket: if you put the paste in an airtight container, it may become soft and even mouldy.

34. Marmellata di Pesche

PEACH JAM

Sicilians call peaches persiche: they are said to have been introduced into Italy from Persia in the classical period. They are produced in abundance, and are usually very cheap in early summer, which is why the nuns most often made peach jam for use in their tarts.

1.8 kg well-ripened peaches
1.2 to 1.5 kg sugar
1 lemon, scrubbed, sliced and seeded

Peel the peaches and cut into 1-cm pieces, discarding the skin and stones. Weigh the peaches and place in a large pot. Add from three-quarters to their entire weight in sugar. Add the lemon slices and stir.

Cook over low heat, stirring occasionally, until the sugar dissolves. Increase the heat and bring to a boil. Then reduce the heat and simmer, stirring often to prevent sticking, for about 30 to 40 minutes: the jam should be thick enough to run off a metal spoon in a ribbon rather than in drops, and a little bit dropped on a plate should spread only slightly.

Skim off any foam and discard the lemon slices. Ladle into hot sterilized jars and seal. Store in a dark place.

THIS MAKES FIVE TO SIX 250-ML JARS OF JAM

35. Marmellata di Arance I

ORANGE MARMALADE I

*Maria makes two different kinds of orange marmalade. This recipe,
the one she uses for marmalade to sell in jars, follows the traditional
Sicilian procedure for preserving citrus fruits, that of soaking the
fruit whole for a few days. Don't be alarmed if it tastes very bitter
when you are cooking it: this will pass as it ages.*

1.5 kg juice oranges (about 9 large oranges)
1.5 kg sugar

Scrub the oranges and prick all over with a fork. Put them in a bowl with water to cover and let soak for 4 days, changing the water every day. Then cut off a tiny piece of skin and taste; if it is still bitter, soak for another day and test again.

Drain the oranges, quarter them, and remove the seeds. Grind the oranges, skin and all, in a meat grinder, using the fine blade.

Combine the orange pulp and sugar in a large non-aluminium pot and cook over low heat, stirring constantly, until the sugar dissolves. Increase the heat, bring to a boil, then reduce the heat and simmer, stirring constantly until the jam is fairly thick and does not run off the spoon.

Spoon into hot sterilized jars, and seal. Store in a cool, dark place for at least 1 month before using.

THIS MAKES SIX 250-ML JARS OF JAM

36. Marmellata di Arance II
ORANGE MARMALADE II

This is the orange marmalade Maria prefers to use for making crostate. It is a little bland for our taste, so use the freshest, most acidic oranges you can find. It was the discarded peels from this recipe that the nuns used in place of whole oranges for making Palline all'Arancia (page 146).

1.5 kg juice oranges
1 kg sugar

Peel the oranges, removing as much of the white pith as possible. Use a small serrated knife to scrape off any remaining pith. Quarter the oranges and remove the seeds. Cut into smaller pieces and grind in a meat grinder, using the fine blade. (Or, using a serrated knife, cut each quarter lengthwise in half and cut each wedge crosswise into very thin slices.)

Weigh the oranges and place in a large non-aluminium pot. Add an equal amount of sugar by weight, and stir well. Cook over low heat, stirring occasionally, until the sugar dissolves. Increase the heat and bring to a boil, then reduce the heat to a simmer, and cook, stirring often to prevent sticking, for about 40 minutes: the marmalade should be thick enough to run off a metal spoon in a ribbon rather than drops, and a little bit dropped on a plate should hold its shape.

Skim off any foam. Ladle into hot sterilized jars and seal. Store in a cool, dark place for at least 1 month before using.

THIS MAKES FIVE 250-ML JARS OF MARMALADE

37. Rosolio alle More
BLACKBERRY CORDIAL

The nuns at the San Carlo would have served this as a cordial, putting a few of the berries in each glass, and would no doubt have considered it a sin of gluttony to think about spooning it over ice cream.

½ kg wild blackberries
300 ml vodka

SYRUP

400 g sugar
400 ml water

Rinse the blackberries lightly, and discard any stems. Put them into a glass jar, add the vodka, and seal tightly. Let stand in a cool, dark place for 8 days.

Combine the sugar and water in a large saucepan and bring to a boil, stirring until the sugar is completely dissolved. Remove from the heat and allow to cool.

Add the vodka and berries to the syrup. Pour into bottles and seal. Let stand in a cool, dark place for at least 2 months before serving.

THIS MAKES 1.5 LTRS OF CORDIAL

38. Rosolio alle Erbe

HERB CORDIAL

Those who saw the movie The Leopard *may remember the scene set on the night of the plebiscite in Donnafugata, when Don Calogero Sedàra offers Prince Fabrizio a tray of tiny glasses of red, white, and green rosolio in the colours of the new Italian flag. This was the same rosolio the nuns made for weddings: it comes in many colours and flavours, some of them quite bilious, especially when they are made with commercial powders. The nuns of the San Carlo (and many centuries of nuns and monks before them) made their cordials from fresh ingredients, and the results are really quite lovely. My favourite is* rosolio alle erbe: *it may be difficult to find the fresh herbs (the lemon verbena used in Italy is the European variety,* Lippia citriodora kunst, *not the American,* Aloysia triphylla)*, but it is worth the effort.*

25 fresh lemon verbena leaves
20 fresh bay leaves
3 to 4 fresh mint leaves
2 to 3 cloves
One 2-cm piece cinnamon stick
1 large piece lemon rind
1 ltr vodka

SYRUP

1.3 kg sugar
1.3 ltrs water

Put the herbs and spices in a jar, add the vodka, cover tightly, and let stand in a cool, dark place for 2 weeks.

Combine the sugar and water in a large saucepan and bring to a boil, stirring until the sugar is completely dissolved. Remove from the heat and allow to cool.

Strain the vodka through a fine-mesh sieve or muslin, discarding the herbs and spices, and add it to the syrup. Cover tightly and allow to stand for 8 days. Strain the cordial through a coffee filter to remove any green deposit that may have risen to the surface, and pour into bottles. Cork tightly.

THIS MAKES 3 LTRS OF CORDIAL

Note: Like many alcoholic drinks, rosolio improves with age. According to a nun quoted in Sebastiana Papa's book on convent cookery, it takes an entire lifetime to make a good nun and 9 months to make a good rosolio. Maria says 2 months will do.

39. Rosolio agli Agrumi
CITRUS CORDIAL

*Maria makes four different citrus cordials, all of which follow the
same procedure. Here as in all recipes calling for citrus peel, it is
important to use the most recently picked fruit that you can find,
and preferably fruit which has been organically grown. The skin of
citrus fruit is quick to absorb pesticides and equally quick, as soon
as it is picked, to lose its essential oils.*

**4 lemons, 4 oranges, 2 large or 3 small grapefruit, or
 6 large tangerines**
300 ml vodka

SYRUP

400 g sugar
400 ml water

Scrub the fruit, and cut away any ink stamps. If you are using lemons, oranges, or grapefruit, cut the peel off as thin as you can, using a swivel-blade peeler or a very sharp knife, so that you have just the coloured zest without the white pith. If using tangerines, peel carefully and remove any white filaments. Save the citrus pulp for another purpose.

Put the peel into a glass jar, add the vodka, and cover tightly. Let stand in a cool, dark place for 2 weeks.

Combine the sugar and water in a large saucepan and bring to a boil, stirring until the sugar is completely dissolved. Remove from the heat and allow to cool.

Strain the vodka through a fine sieve and add it to the syrup. Cover tightly and allow to stand in a cool, dark place for 8 days. Strain the cordial, using a paper coffee filter, to remove any scum that may have formed on the surface, and pour into bottles. Cork tightly. Let stand for 2 months before serving.

THIS MAKES 1 LTR OF CORDIAL

40. Cassatedde di Ricotta
FRIED RICOTTA TURNOVERS

These were a very special treat in the Grammatico household. For most feast days, Maria's mother made cassatedde con la ricotta bollite, a sort of ravioli, with a savoury filling of ricotta seasoned with finely chopped parsley and, when she could spare it, an egg in the pasta dough. These sweet cassatedde were a real extravagance, since sugar had to be bought and frying consumed precious lard.

Some of my friends use pasta machines to roll this dough out into a long strip, as if they were making lasagne, which they then cut into squares and proceed to fill, fold over, and seal as directed.

PASTRY

250 g durum wheat flour
250 g plain flour
65 g sugar
2 tablespoons margarine, melted
2 tablespoons olive oil
1 1/2 teaspoons wine vinegar, any variety
1 tablespoon brandy
Grated zest of 1/2 lemon
175 ml water, or as needed

FILLING

1/2 recipe Crema di Ricotta (page 128)
50 g dark chocolate chips
1/8 teaspoon ground cinnamon
1 egg white, lightly beaten with 1 teaspoon water
1.25 ltrs vegetable oil, for frying

Process the durum wheat flour in a food processor until fine and silky to the touch, about 5 minutes.

Blend the two flours and the sugar together in a bowl or on a work surface, and make a well in the centre. Add the margarine, oil, vinegar, brandy, and lemon zest to the well. Rub the mixture lightly between the palms of your hands until the fat is well incorporated. Add just enough water to make the dough stick together. Press together into a ball, and wrap in cling film or greaseproof paper. Refrigerate while you make the filling and start heating the oil. The oil should be about 7 cm deep in the pan.

Put the ricotta cream in a small bowl and stir in the chocolate chips and cinnamon.

Divide the dough into 12 portions. Knead each one until smooth and then roll it out into a circle about 12 cm in diameter and ¼ cm thick. Place about 2 tablespoons of the filling on the bottom half of each circle, wet the edge with the beaten egg, fold the top half over, and press to seal. Trim the sealed edge with a pastry wheel.

When the oil registers 185°C (365°F) on a cooking thermometer or when a bit of dough dropped in the oil immediately sizzles, add 2 or 3 of the turnovers; do not crowd. Fry until deep golden brown, about 8 minutes. Remove and drain on brown paper or paper towels. Bring the oil back to 185°C (365°F) before adding each batch. Serve warm.

THIS MAKES 12 TURNOVERS

41. Cannoli

Cannoli have followed on the heels of Sicilian emigrants and gained worldwide fame, so much so that Maria is obliged to make them even though they aren't one of her specialities. She keeps ready-made cannoli shells on hand all year round in case someone insists on them, and always makes them according to the old San Carlo recipe at Carnival, when cannoli are de rigueur.

250 g durum wheat flour
250 g plain flour
1½ teaspoons sugar or honey
½ teaspoon unsweetened cocoa powder
100 g lard or margarine, cut into pieces
1½ teaspoons vinegar
1 teaspoon vanilla extract
125 ml water, or as needed
1 egg white, lightly beaten with 1 teaspoon water
1.25 ltrs vegetable oil, for frying
1½ times the recipe Crema di Ricotta (page 128)

Process the durum wheat flour in a food processor until fine and silky to the touch, about 5 minutes.

Combine both flours, the sugar, if using, and cocoa powder in a large mixing bowl. Cut in the lard or margarine, using a pastry blender or two knives. Add the vinegar, vanilla, the honey, if using, and just enough water to make the dough stick together. Press together, wrap in cling film or greaseproof paper, and refrigerate for 30 minutes. (You can make this dough in a food processor, following the directions for Pasta Frolla on page 122.)

To make the cannoli shells, divide the dough into 4 portions. Knead each piece and roll it out into a strip about 40 x 13 x ¼ cm thick. With a template and a pastry wheel, cut out large ovals about 12 x 8 cm. Place a cannoli tube down the length of each oval, bring the sides up and over, and seal with the beaten egg.

Heat the oil in a deep fryer to 185°C (365°F): a piece of pastry dropped into the oil should sizzle immediately. The oil should be 7 to 10 cm deep. Fry the cannoli, a few at a time, until golden brown, about 10 minutes; do not crowd. Remove and drain briefly on brown paper or kitchen towels. Bring the oil back to 185°C (365°F) before adding each batch. Remove the tubes while the cannoli are still warm by grasping each shell in one hand, protected by several layers of kitchen towels, and turning and pulling the tube out gently with the other, using a pot holder or tongs. Allow the cannoli to cool thoroughly.

Just before serving, fill the cannoli shells: the easiest way to do this is to use a piping bag fitted with a large plain nozzle. (Unfilled shells can be stored in an airtight container for up to a week.)

THIS MAKES 16 CANNOLI

Note: If you don't have cannoli tubes, a wooden broomstick sawed into 12 cm lengths makes a good substitute.

42. Torta Paradiso
PARADISE CAKE

This cake is fairly well known throughout Italy under a variety of names: the nuns of the San Carlo were not far off the mark in calling it torta paradiso.

TOPPING

125 g whole blanched almonds
125 g sugar
1 egg
1 egg white
½ teaspoon almond extract

One 23-cm Pan di Spagna (page 124)

SYRUP

100 ml water
50 g sugar
1 tablespoon rum

2 to 3 tablespoons apricot jam, **Marmellata di Pesche** (page 197), or jam of choice, broken up with a spoon and thinned with a drop of water if necessary

Preheat the oven to 200°C/400°F/Gas Mark 6. Line a baking tray with baking parchment or aluminium foil. If using foil, grease it.

Grind the almonds very fine with a tablespoon or so of the sugar. Transfer the almonds to a bowl and add the rest of the sugar, the egg, egg white, and almond extract. Beat until you have a very soft paste that you can squeeze through a piping nozzle.

Place the cake on the baking tray. Fit a piping bag with a 1-cm open star nozzle and fill it halfway with the almond paste topping. Cover the cake with the topping, making a lattice pattern on the top and swirls on the sides. Bake for 10 to 15 minutes, or until golden. Remove to a rack and cool thoroughly.

To make the syrup, combine the water and sugar and bring to a boil, stirring until the sugar dissolves. Remove from the heat and let cool. Stir in the rum.

When the cake is completely cool, turn it upside down on a plate (or in your hand), and brush the bottom with the syrup. Spread it with a thin layer of jam. Turn the cake, jam side down, onto a cake plate.

THIS MAKES 10 TO 12 SERVINGS

43. Torta Divina

MARBLE CAKE

This cake is always sitting on Maria's counter, on sale by the slice, but it is not a San Carlo recipe. Maria thinks of it as her invention, and calls it 'Divine Cake', but it is basically what we in America know as marble cake.

2½ teaspoons baking powder
3 to 5 tablespoons milk
3 eggs
250 g plain flour
250 g sugar
3 tablespoons canola or corn oil
I teaspoon grated lemon zest
I teaspoon vanilla extract
I tablespoon cocoa powder

Preheat the oven to 190°C/375°F/Gas Mark 5. Butter and flour a 23-cm springform tin.

In a large bowl, dissolve the baking powder in 3 tablespoons milk. Add the eggs, flour, sugar, oil, lemon zest, and vanilla and mix well. This is supposed to be a thick batter, but you may need to add a little milk if it is too stiff to mix. Pour one third of the batter into a small bowl and add the cocoa, blending well.

Pour half the white batter into the prepared tin, tilting the tin so it runs out to the edges. Pour the chocolate batter on top, then pour on the remaining white batter. Let stand for 5 minutes to allow the batter to spread evenly in the tin.

Bake for 30 to 35 minutes, or until golden brown on top; the sides should start to come away from the pan and a cocktail stick inserted near the centre should come out clean. Cool in the tin for 5 minutes. Remove the sides of the tin, invert the cake on a rack, and lift off the bottom of the tin. Cool thoroughly.

THIS MAKES 10 TO 12 SERVINGS

44. Cassata Siciliana

The multi-coloured cassata siciliana, with its elegant topping of carefully arranged crystallized fruit, is certainly one of the most famous and most beautiful of Sicilian sweets, although not necessarily the best. It is very sweet indeed, especially the commercial versions, since the more sugar the pastry shop puts in the ricotta cream filling, the longer the cassata will keep without spoiling.

Although now available all winter long (beware when travelling in Sicily of tasting cassata or cannoli in the hot weather: the ricotta will be frozen or reconstituted), cassata was originally an Easter speciality, the one that was distracting the sixteenth-century nuns during Holy Week. The name 'cassata' is said to derive from the Arabic word qas'at, the special dish with sloping sides that was traditionally used to mould the cake.

One 23-cm Pan di Spagna (page 124)
Green food colouring
½ recipe Pasta di Mandorla (page 118)
1 recipe Crema di Ricotta (page 128)

ICING

115 g icing sugar
Juice of ½ lemon

Crystallized fruit for decoration

Slice the cake in half horizontally so there are two layers.

Line a 6-cm deep 23-cm pie dish or other tin with sloping sides with cling film or greaseproof paper, using a dab of jam to 'glue' the paper in place.

Work a few drops of green food colouring into the almond paste, kneading until it becomes a uniform green of medium intensity. Roll the paste out into a narrow strip about 1 cm thick and long enough to line the sides of the dish. Ease the strip into place along the sides of the dish. You may find it easier to handle if you cut the strip into two or three lengths, put them in place one at a time, and then join the ends by pressing gently. Cut off any excess paste with a knife.

Place one of the Pan di Spagna layers on the bottom of the dish, trimming it to fit if necessary. Cut the other layer into ½-cm strips. Use some of these to line the almond paste on the sides of the dish. (This lining serves to keep the ricotta filling from coming into contact with the almond paste and making it gooey; it is not necessary if the cake is to be eaten within a couple of hours.)

Spoon the ricotta cream into the dish, and spread it gently to make an even layer. Crumble the remaining Pan di Spagna strips and any trimmings into small pieces and sprinkle them over the ricotta. Refrigerate.

To make the icing, sift half of the icing sugar into a small bowl. Add the lemon juice and mix until you have a smooth paste. Sift the rest of the sugar into the paste, blending it well as you go. Add water as necessary, drop by drop, mixing continually until you have eliminated any lumps and the icing is shiny and the consistency of a thick syrup.

Turn the cassata upside down onto a serving plate. Carefully remove the dish and the cling film or greaseproof lining. Spread the top and sides with a thin, translucent layer of icing – the green of the paste should show through. Decorate the top with pieces of crystallized fruit arranged in a pleasing design.

Refrigerate for at least 2 hours, or until serving time.

THIS MAKES 10 TO 12 SERVINGS

Note: In the shop, Maria, mindful perhaps of the hours spent beating 'sugar on the slab', now uses commercially prepared fondant to ice her cassate. The above recipe for icing was kindly given to me by Anna Tasca Lanza.

45. Sfinci di Natale
CHRISTMAS FRITTERS

Sfinci (the word is supposed to come from sfang, *an Arabic word meaning 'fried pastry') appear in varying guises on different Sicilian feast days. For St Joseph's Day, they are filled with ricotta cream, and are devastating. This Christmas version from Erice is quite restrained in comparison, although Maria once made me a variation on these sfinci, using part flour and part mashed potatoes. They were every bit as heavy as they sound.*

7 g dry yeast
1½ teaspoons sugar
125 ml lukewarm water
500 g durum wheat flour
7 tablespoons Marsala or stravecchio wine
1½ teaspoons aniseeds
1½ teaspoons grated orange zest (½ orange)
¼ ltr warm milk, or as needed
1.25 ltrs vegetable oil, for frying
130 g sugar mixed with 1 teaspoon ground cinnamon

In a small dish, dissolve the yeast with the sugar in the warm water.

Process the durum wheat flour in a food processor until fine and silky to the touch, about 5 minutes.

Place the flour in a large bowl or the bowl of an electric mixer, and make a well in the centre. Add the dissolved yeast, wine, aniseeds, and grated orange zest. Pour a little of the milk into the dish in which you dissolved the yeast, swish it around to clean the sides, and add to the flour. With a wooden spoon, or the paddle attachment, beat in as much milk as needed to make a fairly soft, elastic dough. Then beat hard until the dough comes away from the sides of the bowl. Allow the dough to rest, loosely covered, until it has doubled in volume, about 1 hour.

Heat 5 to 7 cm of oil in a large deep saucepan or deep fryer to 185°C (365°F); a bit of dough dropped in the oil should dance around and sizzle. Wet your fingers, pull off pieces of dough no larger than a walnut, and drop into the hot oil; do not crowd. The sfinci will turn over by themselves in the oil; when they are deep golden all over, about 10 minutes, remove with a slotted spoon and drain on brown paper or paper towels. Bring the oil back to 185°C (365°F) before adding each batch. Roll the fried sfinci in the cinnamon sugar, and serve warm.

THIS MAKES ABOUT 35 SFINCI

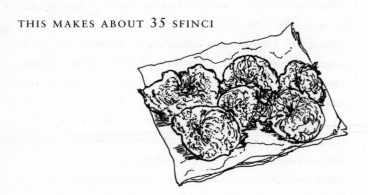

Note: Sicilians usually use stick cinnamon, freshly ground in a mortar or a coffee grinder, in their cooking, and it is noticeably better than store-bought ground cinnamon.

46. Polpette Dolci
SWEET MEATBALLS

This recipe for polpette dolci, one of Maria's favourite dishes when she was at the San Carlo, must be extremely old, for it has that curious mixture of savoury and sweet that was very popular throughout Europe in the Renaissance and still lingers in odd corners of the Sicilian cuisine. I have never seen any other polpette recipe that calls for ground almonds – which, together with the abundant cinnamon, give these meatballs their delicious and very distinctive flavour.

Like most meatballs or fishballs made in the Trapani area, these should be made with pine nuts and currants – luxury items the nuns at the San Carlo never purchased. They would dry and chop the grapes that weren't perfect enough to preserve in spirits, and then would send the Auntie down to gather pine cones in the woods below Erice for their nuts. In their thrift, they also used almost twice as many breadcrumbs as this recipe suggests, thus making the meat go twice as far.

The meatballs are cooked in a tomato sauce and should be served with pasta.

SAUCE

1 small onion, chopped
1 clove garlic, minced
2 tablespoons olive oil
1 tablespoon tomato purée
125 ml warm water
675 ml passata
One 2-cm piece cinnamon stick
½ teaspoon salt
¼ teaspoon freshly ground black pepper

MEATBALLS

150 g whole blanched almonds, toasted
1 tablespoon sugar
450 g minced beef
200 g stale white breadcrumbs (made, if possible, from
     Italian bread with crusts removed)
100 g freshly grated pecorino cheese
30 g currants
30 g pine nuts
One 7-cm piece cinnamon stick, ground (1 teaspoon)
1 teaspoon salt
¼ teaspoon freshly ground black pepper
2 to 3 eggs
Olive or vegetable oil for sautéing

To prepare the sauce, sauté the onion and garlic in the olive oil until translucent but not coloured. Add the tomato purée and warm water, stirring to dissolve it. Simmer for 1 minute, then add the passata, cinnamon stick, salt, and pepper, and simmer for 15 minutes.

Meanwhile, prepare the meatballs. Grind the almonds with the sugar. Combine the ground nuts with the beef, breadcrumbs, cheese, currants, pine nuts, cinnamon, salt, and pepper, and mix well. Add as many eggs as you need to bind the mixture. Shape into 3-cm balls or patties, and brown in the oil.

Add the meatballs to the simmering sauce. Simmer about 20 minutes, or until the meatballs are cooked through.

THIS MAKES 8 SERVINGS

Bibliography

Adragna, Vincenzo. *Erice*. Trapani, 1987.

Castronovo, Giuseppe. *Erice oggi Monte San Giuliano*. 3 vols. Palermo, 1880.

——. *Erice sacra*, manuscript copy of unpublished nineteenth-century work. Biblioteca Comunale, Erice.

di Carpegna, Cristina. *I monasteri: agricoltura e artigianato alimentare*. In Istituto Nazionale di Sociologia Rurale, ed., *Gastronomia e società*. Milano, 1984.

Field, Carol. *Celebrating Italy*. New York, 1990.

Fraga Iribarne, Maria Luisa. *Guia de dulces de los conventos sevillanos de clausura*. Còrdoba, 1988.

Italia, Antonio. *La Sicilia feudale*. Genova, Roma, Napoli, 1940.

Lanza, Anna Tasca. *The Heart of Sicily: Recipes and Reminiscences of Regaleali*. New York, 1993.

Levi, Carlo. *Le pietre sono parole*. Torino, 1964.

Lo Monte, Mimmetta. *Classic Sicilian Cooking*. New York, 1990.

Malgieri, Nick. *Great Italian Desserts*. Boston, 1990.

Papa, Sebastiana. *La nuova cucina dei monasteri*. Milano, 1993.

Simeti, Mary Taylor. *On Persephone's Island: A Sicilian Journal*. New York, 1986 (reissued London, 2001).

——. *Pomp and Sustenance: Twenty-Five Centuries of Sicilian Food*. New York, 1989 (reissued London, 1999).

——. 'The Almond Pastries of Erice'. In *Gourmet*, Vol. LI, N.11. November, 1991.

Uccello, Antonino. *Pani e dolci di Sicilia*. Palermo, 1976.

Zarri, Gabriella. *Monasteri femminili e città (secoli XV–XVIII)*. In AAVV., *Storia d'Italia, Annali*, Vol. 9. Torino, 1986. pp. 359–429.

Index